MADE BY JAMES

MADE BY JAMES

THE HONEST GUIDE TO CREATIVITY AND LOGO DESIGN

JAMES MARTIN

ROCKPORT

Quarto.com

© 2021 Quarto Publishing Group USA Inc.

Text and images © 2021 James Martin

First published in 2021 by Rockport Publishers, an imprint of The Quarto Group,
100 Cummings Center, Suite 265-D, Beverly, MA 01915, USA.
T (978) 282-9590 F (978) 283-2742

Rockport Publishers titles are also available at discount for retail, wholesale, promotional, and bulk purchase. For details, contact the Special Sales Manager by email at specialsales@quarto.com or by mail at The Quarto Group, Attn: Special Sales Manager, 100 Cummings Center, Suite 265-D, Beverly, MA 01915, USA.

10 9 8 7 6 5 4

ISBN: 978-0-7603-7149-7

Digital edition published in 2021

eISBN: 978-0-76037-150-3

Library of Congress Cataloging-in-Publication Data

Names: Martin, James, 1983- author.

Title: Made by James : the honest guide to creativity and logo design / James Martin.

Description: Beverly, MA : Rockport Publishers, 2021. | Includes index.

Identifiers: LCCN 2021018401 (print) | LCCN 2021018402 (ebook) | ISBN 9780760371497 (hardcover) | ISBN 9780760371503 (ebook)

Subjects: LCSH: Logos (Symbols)--Design.

Classification: LCC NC1002.L63 M377 2021 (print) | LCC NC1002.L63 (ebook) | DDC 741.6--dc23

LC record available at https://lccn.loc.gov/2021018401

LC ebook record available at https://lccn.loc.gov/2021018402

Design: Jason Tselentis
Page Layout: Mattie Wells

Printed in China

DEDICATION

This book is dedicated to all my fellow creatives, no matter how long you've been in the industry. Together we can keep our creative community strong, and let's always aim to inspire others. Respect to you all.

Mum, Dad, Chris, Kate, and Bucky—I love ya.

CONTENTS

now and again. So how on earth is this all happening?

I find great solace in being uncomfortable; I don't like comfort zones, and I love doing things that take me out of them . . . like this. That being said, I have the opportunity to help my fellow designers more than ever before. The fact that there are crazy people in the world, like me, who feel a book written from my brain is something the world needs makes me super scared and crazy happy—but more importantly, unbelievably proud.

My aim is to fill this book with as much value as possible to help you become whatever you desire in the creative world. I want this book to be your best mate in the good times and the bad. Because let's be honest: things don't always go the way we want them to.

I didn't write this book to dictate what you should be doing (I'm still figuring that out myself), but I did write it to be a guide you can turn to when you need it.

▮ LET ME PROPERLY INTRODUCE MYSELF

My name is James Martin. I'm a bearded designer fool from the south coast of the United Kingdom. A lot of you may know me as Made by James through social media, that crazy world we all dip in and out of on the daily. I run my design agency, Baby Giant Design Co., with my great friend Ady Matengu. We made a big decision all that time ago to venture off from an agency together and our patience and persistence have rewarded us in so many ways.

I started my Instagram account in 2012, and for a long time I posted pictures of fires and my dog; I thought that's what the 'gram was all about. I later read the book *Show Your Work,* by Austin Kleon, and from that day forward I decided to use my Instagram account to . . . show my work. That's probably the day that led to this moment we're sharing together now.

Today Made by James has become something bigger than I could have ever imagined. In fact, it's become larger than just me. My platform is now a community, a team of designers and non-designers, of all ages from around the globe. It's a place to learn and, more importantly, a place where we can all talk about the good and the bad in our lives, honestly.

I would often joke to my friends, while slightly tipsy on some alcoholic beverage, "I will write a book one day!" They would ask, "What on?" and I would make something up because I really didn't have an answer.

Jokes aside, I have always wanted to write a book but never thought it would happen. When I received a message from a book editor, I thought it was spam and almost deleted it. Luckily I stopped myself before potentially making the biggest mistake I could have made to date. And trust me, I have made a few.

While you're reading this book, I want you to remember a couple of things. The first thing is that you and I have a lot in common. We all start our journey somewhere and we all want to make something of ourselves. For some it takes years, and for others, decades. Remember that even a tiny step toward your goal every day is a step in the right direction. Good things take time.

The second thing I want you to remember is to never let anyone tell you that you're not good enough. When I was ten years old, I was in an art class making pottery with a table of friends. We were no doubt being a little loud, messing around a bit, and generally being ten years old. My art teacher walked up to me, picked up the clay pig I was making, and chucked it into the trash. This was swiftly followed by the words, "You will never make any money out of art."

NEEDLESS TO SAY, SHE WAS WRONG.

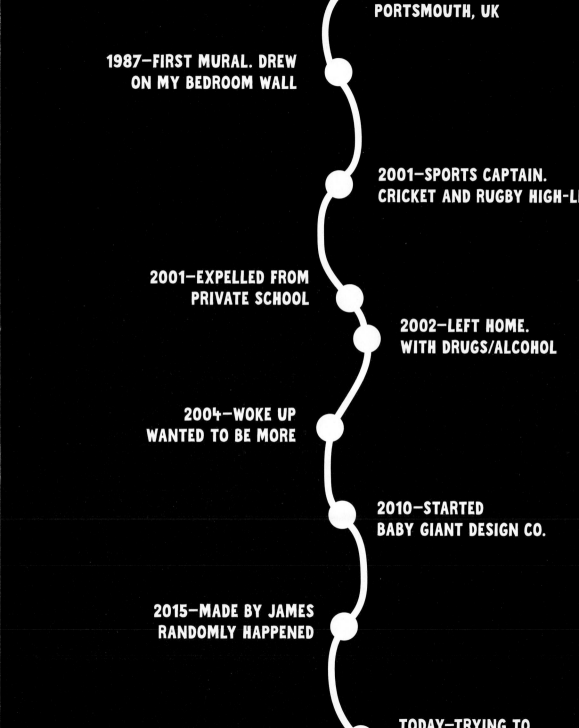

PORTSMOUTH, UK

1987—FIRST MURAL. DREW
ON MY BEDROOM WALL

2001—SPORTS CAPTAIN.
CRICKET AND RUGBY HIGH-LI

2001—EXPELLED FROM
PRIVATE SCHOOL

2002—LEFT HOME.
WITH DRUGS/ALCOHOL

2004—WOKE UP
WANTED TO BE MORE

2010—STARTED
BABY GIANT DESIGN CO.

2015—MADE BY JAMES
RANDOMLY HAPPENED

TODAY—TRYING TO

▌ WHAT YOU CAN EXPECT FROM THIS BOOK

Over the next couple of hundred pages, I will hold nothing back. But I won't be using this opportunity to blow my own trumpet and tell you how amazing I am. My mum does that every day, so we have that covered.

We are human, and we all mess up. Life isn't a wonderfully organized journey that works out exactly the way we want it to. It's a bendy path of discovery and errors. Life, like design, is a process, one we're always looking to tweak and change until we find something that works.

This is the book I wish I had growing up as a human and a creative, and I hope I have filled it with most of what you need to find solace in bad times and create action in good times. So, I suppose I will stop babbling and let you get on with reading it!

WHAT INSPIRED MY CREATIVE JOURNEY

At the age of four, I created my first mural, a masterpiece with crayons on the bedroom wall, done with the finesse of a baby giraffe. I always doodled as a kid and found the process of creating something from nothing truly fascinating.

In my teens I developed a massive admiration for skateboard culture, and then in my late teens and early twenties my love of tattoo art grew. All of this has had a formative impact on my process. I love the mixture of typographic elements and combinations of illustrations that come together to tell a story.

I'll go into more detail about my life over the course of this book, but this gives you an idea of how creativity has always been prevalent in my life, and how it all started with a simple red crayon and a ruined bedroom wall. Sorry, Mum and Dad—my bad.

1 THE PAST, PRESENT, AND FUTURE

This chapter is full of all the stuff that made me the person I am today, the good and the bad, but all of it important. We tend to see and hear just the good stuff in people's lives, but I'll be talking you through my journey as a young boy, through my troubled teens, and through having to restart with a clean slate as a young adult.

What I hope you gain from this chapter is that it's okay to make mistakes, and sometimes things happen that are out of your control. The most important thing is what you do today and tomorrow—that's the stuff that really matters.

Your past does not define you, but it can help make you.

THE EARLY YEARS

I have only wonderful memories of growing up. My brother, Chris Martin, and I were always playing outside and being taken on adventures with Mum and Dad, often with a group of friends and their parents. Holidays were all about the outdoors: camping and adventures in the woods, making bows and arrows out of branches, and bracken dens to shelter from the cold weather. These also doubled up as fantastic hiding places for a game of hide and seek.

This period in my life, I see now, was a great driving force for my creativity. All of those hours spent outside exploring and making something from nothing were awesome. I can take this bracken and make shelter; I can take this branch and make a weapon. Something can easily be created if you use your imagination.

This is why I still love the outdoors and have the imagination of a six year old. This was a time of discovery, endless opportunities, and creativity. As we get older, we are taught to be more responsible and grow up, and in most scenarios, this is the right thing to do. I've always viewed it differently (my dad constantly reminds me that I live on a different planet) because I still carry that sense of adventure that allows me to think a little differently. I don't fear being wrong; I fear not trying something.

LITTLE TIP

Some of the biggest discoveries in history have been found while at play. When you lose your childish sense of adventure, you kill your creativity. Go play.

" THEY TAUGHT ME TO HUSTLE BEFORE IT WAS A SOCIAL MEDIA HASHTAG. "

A strong work ethic is another key attribute I learned from a young age. Each weekday, Mum would pick me and my brother up from school and then go pick up Dad from work. If my Mum was working, then Dad would pick us all up. They both worked all the hours that the day gave them. Mum, a nurse, often worked nights, and Dad traveled to dangerous parts of the world for work to make money for our family. That work ethic didn't exclude me and my brother. On weekends we would not be allowed to sit in front of the television; we would be asked to help in the garden, rake the leaves, or push around the wheelbarrow.

Obviously, we hated these chores as kids, but my parents taught us a valuable lesson: rest and watching TV were rewards for effort. The weird thing is that now I struggle to sit and watch TV. I greatly prefer finding jobs to do in the garden. They taught me how to hustle before it was a social media hashtag. Thanks, Mum and Dad. Love ya.

▌EDUCATION

I was extremely lucky with my education. I was not the brightest student, but I loved the social side to school and all the activities and sports. The one thing I miss from school in my day-to-day routine today is that team player mentality. I loved being a part of a team and how everyone had each other's back on the rugby field. This is why I still play cricket, maybe not as well as I used to and often after a beer. But I still love the competition, camaraderie, and the idea that you're a part of something.

This is also why I hold the creative community so dear to me now. This community is passionate, positive, and it pushes me forward. Most people who write books like this do it once they have retired and their thoughts are based on a world from twenty years ago. The fact that I am writing this book while "in the trenches" with this community gives me a sense of responsibility to tell them the honest truth about the day-to-day running of a design business.

"

I REBELLED BIG TIME. I WENT FROM A PRIVATELY EDUCATED SPORTS CAPTAIN TO A DROPOUT AND WASTE OF SPACE WITHIN A COUPLE OF YEARS

"

I especially enjoyed art and design lessons in school. I was not the best student by a long shot, but whenever I walked into that classroom it felt like a safe space, a place where I could be on an even footing with my friends and classmates. This was one class where I didn't need to hide in the back. Then something happened to me that would change my life forever.

At the age of eleven, I was sexually abused by one of my teachers. Looking back on this moment with slightly wiser eyes, the experience changed my whole life's trajectory in an instant. I don't want to dwell too much on this one incident, because I don't want to give him any more of my time—he has taken away far too much of that. The reason I share this with you is because it's something real that happened in my life and contributed to the person I am today.

Throughout your life you will encounter hurdles and stumbling blocks. Some may feel impossible to get over, but I promise you that with time they do get better, or more often you find a way to deal with them in a more positive manner. It took me almost seven years before I told anybody about what happened.

This incident changed everything for me. I no longer respected any sort of authority, which made me fall out with my parents, ignore all my teachers at school, and I lost a lot of friends who always had my back. I thought the world was against me and I needed to shut everyone out to feel safe. As a result, I developed a drug problem from the age of about sixteen, which subsequently got me expelled from school for theft and drug-related problems.

My life began with so much promise—I was enrolled at great schools and had endless opportunities—but it ended in no A levels (required exams that would allow me to attend university), no direction, and no clue. At age seventeen, I went off the rails and left home to start my own life away from it all. I'll never use what happened to me as an excuse for the way I behaved; we all deal with stuff differently.

I rebelled big time. I went from a privately educated sports captain to a dropout and waste of space within a couple of years. I try to forget these years, but I also use them as learning tools every day.

BEFORE I BECAME A (REAL) GRAPHIC DESIGNER

It took me a few years to find what I wanted to do for the rest of my life. After getting kicked out of school and leaving home, I was pretty much starting from nothing, which meant I could be whatever I wanted to be. Unfortunately, I took great advantage of this. I found jobs to pay for my rent and support my drug and partying habits—not a sustainable or clever use of time.

After two years of this I finally woke up, both physically and mentally. The cliché of waking up one day and changing my life was exactly what happened. I woke up one morning and said to myself, "What the hell am I doing with my life?" I knew the answer and I had to change it.

Art and creativity were the only things I enjoyed enough to pursue. It was a way for me to kick-start my life again. I never knew it would lead me here, but I knew I needed to do something to get me out of a rut. A few days later I enrolled in the local college to do a yearlong art foundation course, learning about everything from fine arts to sculpture and textiles to graphic design, and this is when my life restarted. I had focus, I had a plan, and more importantly, I was starting to find myself again. I quickly became that little kid again, playing in the woods and leading my rugby team to success. I started to enjoy waking up again. After completing the art foundation course, my tutor mentioned that I should consider graphic design as a possible career path. I had no clue what this was at the time but thought, "Why not give it a go?" I had nothing to lose.

While continuing my design education to earn a two-year higher national diploma in graphic design, I also dipped my toe into other bits and bobs, like teaching art for a year and completing a tattoo apprenticeship under the artist who created my tattoos at the time. I felt a spark for my love of drawing again and I got into illustration and art, creating daily doodles of crazy characters in my sketchbook. The process of creating was back in my life, and I loved it.

My love of teaching has always been a part of me, but I felt the timing wasn't right—I was still trying to figure myself out, so how could I teach others? I continued with the graphic design direction and now, fifteen years later, I'm writing this book about logo design and my crazy creative journey. Weird how things have worked out.

LITTLE TIP

Don't rush your career choices. If there's something you want to try, you have way more time than you think, so be patient and follow your own path. Remember that slow progress is still progress.

While at university I decided to get some work experience, so I would literally knock on design studio doors and ask if they had any open positions. Although it wasn't a successful tactic, the fact that I tried made me certain that this was what I wanted to do.

One day while I was working in a local café, a customer who knew I wanted to be a designer approached me. His friend ran a small design agency, and they were looking for new designers to join the team. You may think that's luck, but I call it years of hard work trying to get my life back. Let's call it a lucky reward for the effort.

DESIGN SCHOOL OR NO DESIGN SCHOOL?

The question I get asked the most is, "Do I need to go to design school to be a designer?"

It's important not to use formal education as a barrier to become whatever you want to be. The key to success is your drive and passion for any given subject. Don't let the experiences of others cloud your judgment.

Here are a few benefits for each choice. I always like to think of the positives rather than distract myself with the negatives.

MY PROS FOR DESIGN SCHOOL:

* You are typically assigned a teacher who can help guide you
* You learn the importance of working with deadlines
* You learn the importance of showing up for yourself
* You get to interact with like-minded people

MY PROS FOR NOT GOING TO DESIGN SCHOOL:

* You can save a lot of money
* You can practice niche subjects that interest you, like logo design or animation, and be more specific with your education to focus on your preferred area
* You can learn at your own speed

It comes down to your mindset. With the right mindset, you can achieve anything. Whether you enroll in design school or not, I feel we creative types are all self-taught to some degree. We are learning every day, developing our skill sets, and trying to grow as creatives.

I didn't go to "logo school," but I taught myself how to develop my skills in that area with practice and patience. Practice led to work, work led to more work, and I had to be patient. Your work ethic, personality, and portfolio will get you work, not just a piece of paper. A degree is not always mandatory for getting work, especially at agencies.

MY FIRST AGENCY EXPERIENCE

In my last year of university, I started working at a company called Irelish Media. I did everything from making tea and coffee to web design, Photoshop, using Flash to create animation, and general graphic design work. Although I was not great at any of it, I was learning so many new aspects of design, and the job allowed me to start to understand the industry.

This was a massive eye-opener for me. Before starting at the agency in 2005, I was just a creative—with a pick-up-a-pencil-and-draw kind of attitude. Everything changed when I started applying creativity toward work for other people. There was suddenly a little more pressure to perform.

One of the takeaways from my years working in an agency was being able to observe how the business was run. By the time I left, I gained a huge amount of experience in the day-to-day running of a real agency, in the real world, and doing real work for real clients.

I saw what worked and what didn't, I learned how to structure a meeting, how to sell ideas, how to listen to a client's feedback, the process of pricing projects, how to liaise and communicate with clients, and the importance of building relationships with other industry professionals such as printers and sign writers.

The biggest win from all of this was meeting my friend, and now business partner, Ady, lead designer at the time. When the company we were working for was winding down to close, we decided to start our own little agency and see if we could make it by ourselves.

Ady and I realized that with our joint knowledge we could make it work. We knew what to do and how to do it, and by this stage I was not as inexperienced as I once was. The knowledge you gain in an agency will stay with you for life. Being a creative is not enough—you have to know how to turn that creativity into a business that thrives. That's the real trick.

LITTLE TIP

I urge anyone to get some agency work before going freelance. You can observe how the industry works and gain experience in areas other than creativity, such as working with clients and learning the business side of the profession.

BABY GIANT DESIGN CO.

Baby Giant—my beautiful oxymoron.

Before my company Baby Giant Design Co. was even an idea, I was interviewing with other agencies and not getting very far. During one interview I received some of the best feedback that still lives with me to this day. As the interviewer looked through my portfolio he said, "James, in terms of illustration and creativity you are an eight out of ten. In terms of websites you are a three out of ten. Ditch the web stuff and concentrate on being a creative."

At first, I was struck by his brutal honesty, but after pondering it for a few days I realized he was right. My web stuff was awful, and at the same time I also hated doing it. I grew up in an era where I thought being a full-stack designer would be beneficial—the classic jack-of-all-trades and master of none. This interviewer's words made me understand that it was more beneficial to be brilliant at one thing than average at many.

After going on a couple of interviews I started to think about creating something of my own. I loved the idea of working for myself but worried I wouldn't have the security of an agency job that came with regular pay and a steady stream of work. It took a friend to say, "Don't be an idiot, you should do it" for Ady and me to commit and start this little adventure— thanks for the advice, Phil Owen (Phil happens to be my father-in-law).

LITTLE TIP

I started getting loads of referrals from clients when they shared my contact information with their friends and business colleagues. Remember that everything you put out into the world has your name on it, so make sure it's banging.

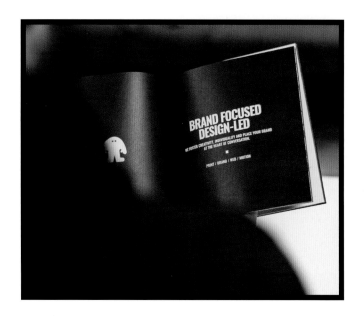

When you start any business you always hope for the best and expect the worst. In 2010, the BGCO adventure started. It wasn't easy. Ady and I managed to scrape a few clients together, but it was tough to gain any real traction in the beginning.

Sometimes we'd do free logo work to earn other work the client would offer. We were trying to get our foot in the door with any company we could; we knew that once we were in, we'd need to seriously mess up to get booted back out. The odd bit of free work was a great way to get a client to trust us.

To keep busy we started new ventures (T-shirt and notebook companies) and anything else we thought we could make a quick buck on. These projects kept us busy, but none of these ever came to anything. We never made much money because we didn't give them the time and effort they needed.

We also spent a lot of time making sure our identity and messaging was cohesive, and we worked on our website and brand constantly to make sure we were aligning ourselves with the clients we wanted to attract.

The business started to change circa 2015. The company was five years old, and momentum was picking up. We had some representation of our work out in the world and that was a great advertising tool. The business began to get a lot of referrals, so we didn't have to pitch for any work. The work evolved from little bits and bobs to bigger and better projects. All that effort we put in to survive in the early years was starting to pay off.

LITTLE TIP

Work when others are working, whether you are busy or not. Ady and I would always work from 9:00 a.m. to 5:00 p.m., five days a week, whether we were doing our own work or client work. When we got busy, it was easy to work regular hours because we already had a set routine.

BLAHZY.

 TODAY, BGCO CONTINUES TO GROW YEAR AFTER YEAR, AND WE HAVE EVEN INVESTED IN OTHER COMPANIES AS SHAREHOLDERS AND PARTNERS. IT'S BEEN A TOUGH, AWESOME, EMOTIONAL, CRAZY, AND INSPIRING JOURNEY SO FAR, AND WE'RE JUST GETTING STARTED. I WOULDN'T CHANGE ANY OF IT. "

MADE BY JAMES

Baby Giant was my baby, so creating a personal brand was never in the game plan. I'm not sure what made me change my Instagram handle from @jamalicious to @made.by.james, but I suppose it was when I decided to take my work a little more seriously that I came up with a more apt name.

I thought sharing my creative process would be a fascinating thing to see. I was always super intrigued by the work of other designers, but you rarely ever get behind the scenes to see how that work is done. My natural inclination to always be a little different from everyone else probably made me rebel against this norm, so I started sharing more and more on social media how I came up with my ideas. Made by James, and the community that has developed around it, has become something much bigger than I could have ever imagined.

Although this sharing was never planned, I do have some advice on building a community of awesome humans, or My Team, as I like to call them. These are all the people who engage with me.

THE FOUR MAIN RULES BY WHICH I GOVERN MYSELF ARE:

▌ CONSISTENCY
▌ HONESTY
▌ AUTHENTICITY
▌ VULNERABILITY

Those who follow me on social media know that these words lead my everyday interactions. I don't pretend to be someone I'm not, and I share my real life with people, even when it's really freaking tough.

My message for anyone interested in starting a personal brand is to show the good and the bad of yourself. People are looking for authenticity, and that genuineness makes you relatable and human. People want to work with people.

The best things to come out of this journey are the people I get to meet and the collaborations I get to work on. Growing up, my dream was to one day be as cool as the dudes over at Lincoln Design Co., who for me are the pinnacle of everything cool in the design world, creating the best work for the best clients, and all done in their own unique style. When I started BGCO, Lincoln Design Co. was a massive source of inspiration. Not only have I now worked with Dan Lincoln and his team on developing my own brand assets for Made by James, but I now get to call them my friends. That's not something I thought would ever happen.

I have no idea what the future holds, but I know that I'll never stop showing up for you, and I will always bring a little bit of real into a world that mostly likes to hide it. I know what my mission is: to help the creatives of this world become whatever they want to be, and to help them find their own voice in a very noisy industry. Although I'm now a logo designer by trade, the information in this book relates to design and creativity as a whole and there's something relatable for everyone.

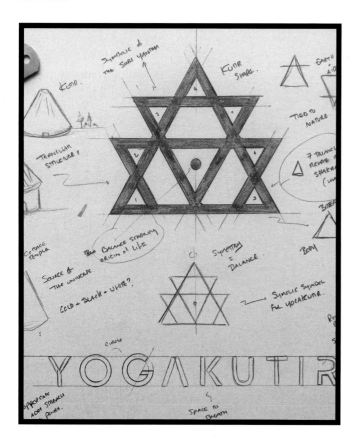

ALWAYS BE POSITIVE, AND CHOOSE YOUR SOURCES WISELY

Growing up I never had a creative guide. My mum and dad were always super supportive of whatever I did, but they'll be the first to tell you they don't have a creative bone in their body. At school, creativity was more "This is how to do it" rather than "Show me how you would do it."

The real world is different. Creativity has become more of a competition than a community. I know how difficult it can be to find accurate information from the right people, especially with the Internet and the noise and opinions being thrown around by people trying to make a quick buck. We are now at a place where people with minimal experience in the design world are teaching people how to design, and that is scary. There are people who have never done agency work telling people to never get agency work. There are people selling courses on subjects they don't have enough knowledge on. Just be sure to research the people who are trying to sell you information before you run your life by it.

My advice to you is this: Be a positive influence in whatever community you are involved in, help others, and ask lots of questions. Don't rely on one source or restrict your learning to one individual. Having a broad knowledge of any subject will help you define what's useful and what isn't. Do your research, choose your sources wisely, and even when you find that perfect formula that works for you, continue to seek wisdom and add your signature to it. Remember that knowledge can only be called knowledge if you share it with others.

" KNOWLEDGE CAN ONLY BE CALLED KNOWLEDGE IF YOU SHARE IT. "

2 CREATING AN EFFECTIVE WORK PROCESS

It's time to drop some knowledge about the things I've learned while developing my work process. I'll jump into some simple ideas that can help you find your style, become more productive, and most importantly, develop a career as a creative. Unfortunately, our industry isn't just about pretty colors and unicorns. We must all make our way in this world, and that means creating good habits and solid routines to allow ourselves to be fully focused on the big picture (pun intended).

This chapter will give you insight into some of the fundamentals when it comes to having an effective day-to-day routine, as well as highlighting the importance of being patient and building longevity in the industry. This is not a bunch of quick fixes—I'm in this for the long haul, and I want you right there with me.

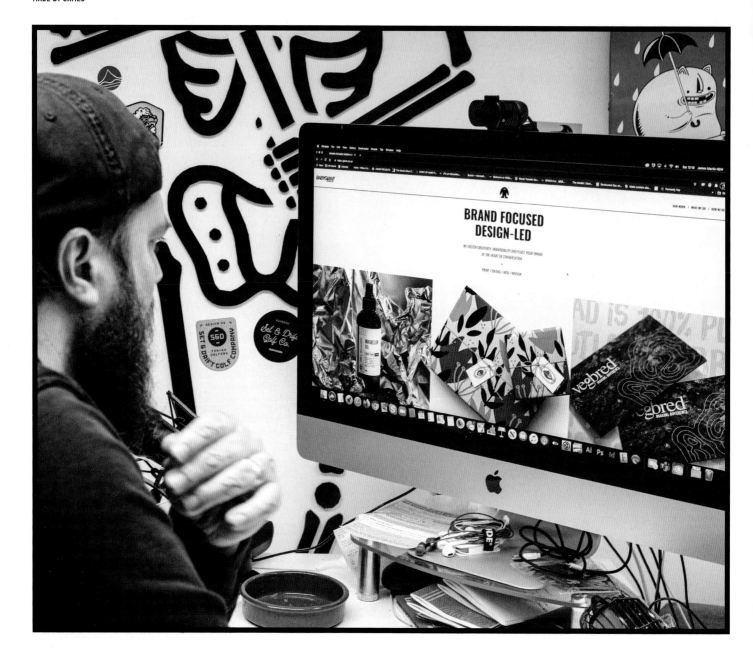

LITTLE TIP

Never see your client as a monetary transaction. That in no way builds a relationship. Don't just think about the first job; think about all the other possible jobs that may come from it. Be helpful to your client and mindful of the future.

▌ HOW TO GAIN CLIENTS

Acquiring clients may be the single most important part of being any kind of working creative. Without paying clients, we are merely hobbyists. The real win is being able to turn our hobby into a long and fruitful career.

As with everything we do, building a client base gets easier over time, so don't worry if you're struggling in the beginning—every designer on the planet has had the same issue. In the very early days at Baby Giant I did a ton of free work for people, or even bartered my services in exchange for theirs. In fact, I still love a bit of a bartering. It makes me feel like a pirate.

The creative mind doesn't have to be restricted to art—you can use it to creatively problem solve any issue you may have, including brainstorming ideas on how to get more work. Here are five ways I've had success gaining clients over the years:

▌ 1. CONFIDENTLY TELL YOUR FRIENDS AND FAMILY YOU ARE A DESIGNER.

Your first client will probably be someone you know, such as a friend or family member. The best thing you can do is tell everyone you know what you do, and make sure they know you are not messing around. The next time they're in need of a designer or talking to someone looking for a designer, I can guarantee your name will be put forward.

▌ 2. INVEST IN YOURSELF AND YOUR ONLINE PRESENCE.

Put effort into making your online presence look solid and trustworthy. Clients do a fair bit of research when looking for a designer, so make sure you give them no reason to doubt your skills. Build a website, ask for reviews from anyone you have done work for, and be active on social media. If you add up all the clothes, shoes, and coffees you've purchased this year, those alone could pay for web hosting and a cool portfolio website.

3. DON'T LOOK AT FREE WORK AS LOST TIME; SEE IT AS A POSSIBLE PATH TO MORE WORK.

I made a logo ten years ago for free, and that has equated to ten years' worth of work ever since with that one client. Sometimes giving a little can get you a lot, so assess the opportunity. If you feel that the original effort you put in can be rewarded back (and some) over time, then go for it. Ultimately you need to go with your gut and do what you feel is best. Free work has to be our choice and I personally only do it when it feels right. As long as you are in control of the decision making, you can make it work.

4. WHY WAIT FOR THEM? GO GET 'EM.

While building a business, work rarely finds you. You have to put yourself out there. Send your work and portfolio to clients you want to work with and let local design agencies know you're available to freelance. Putting yourself out there can bring fantastic results. Even if it comes to nothing, putting yourself out there and trying to make something is more important than not trying anything at all. I'd prefer to drop a few hours into some free work (and have something for my portfolio) rather than sit around waiting for clients to find me. At least by doing work I am learning, gaining experience, and honing my skills. The energy you contribute to your work generates a hustle culture that later creates wins.

5. BARTER LIKE A PIRATE, ME HEARTIES!

I love to barter, exchanging my skills in return for someone else's. You don't always have to work for money—you can get creative and exchange services, value for value. Sometimes the money you'd make from the project would be spent buying a similar product or service anyway.

The most important thing you can do in business and in life is be yourself. The energy you put out into the world will attract the right people and the right clients. Being a good human is more important than being a good designer, and you may find that you've gotten a job over someone more qualified because the client likes you and can envision working with you. Never underestimate the power your personality can bring to the table.

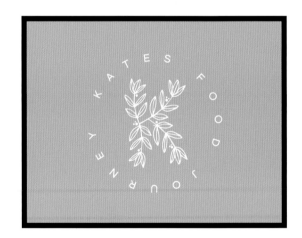

JUST SAY YES—UNTIL YOU HAVE THE LUXURY OF SAYING NO

Back in the day, when I was a little beardless graphic designer, I was always scavenging for work. It's super tough to get work rolling in consistently when you start out, so I learned quickly just to say yes to everything, even if I couldn't do it.

I said yes to everything and would just figure it out. I'd learn how to do it or, in some cases, partner up with people who could do it, and I'd act as the middleman. At the beginning of BGCO, Ady and I were lucky, as we could cover most requests. But if we were asked to do something we had never done or had no clue about, we would still say yes (within reason, of course) and get it sorted out.

This put us in a great position as a young agency, because we became the people to chat to for anything that needed to be designed or created. The people looking to hire would come to us with a job, and if we physically couldn't do it we would find someone who could. We'd act as the project manager and would take a cut on the project.

CAN YOU DO WEB DESIGN? YES.

CAN YOU DESIGN BROCHURES? YES.

CAN YOU DO A MURAL ON OUR WALL? YES.

I believe that turning away work while building your business is a bad move. You are a bright, creative human, so figure out a viable way to make it happen. Saying yes opens so many new opportunities to make money and also helps grow your network and client base. You can also offer a small commission (about 10 percent) to people who bring work your way, giving others the incentive to push work in your direction. This has worked great for me, and everybody wins.

One day you'll get to a stage where you can say no to work that doesn't fit your wheelhouse. Until that day comes, hustle.

LITTLE TIP

A message to all freelancers out there: Buddy up with people who have different skills from you, allowing you to add value to your clients, and form a collective. You can all bring work in and work on projects together when possible or make money on work you might not be able to do by acting as a middleman or project manager.

FINDING YOUR STYLE

Hey, James, how do I find my own style?

This is a big question and one that probably doesn't have a definitive answer, as all artists and creators who have a unique style probably don't know how they managed to find it.

This question actually leads me to different question: Does your style find you? This is a more accurate way to think about capturing your own style. This isn't to say you should sit on the sofa for ten years waiting for someone to figure it out for you—you have to experiment and put your energy into the creative process. But there are some elements that, once popped together, will help you find that elusive style that is craved.

The process is often rushed, and sometimes people are too heavily influenced by others. We've all seen how, for example, someone gets a little traction on the Instagram algorithm by doing a post on how to design carousels for the platform. Suddenly, a similar carousel appears, but in a different color with a different font, but overall, quite similar.

A design style is not developed for popularity or to gain followers on the 'gram. It comes from the way you work, your process, your execution, and, most importantly, your own personality. To truly thrive, a style must be loved and nurtured like anything else—you can't just find a style and work on it once a month. It involves effort, failures, mistakes, and sometimes crying in a corner thinking, will I ever make it? A style is the soul of every creative. When you find it, make sure you take care of it.

YOU CAN DEFINE YOUR OWN STYLE BY BECOMING FAMILIAR WITH THE FOUR P'S:

▌PERSONALITY

You need to have a solid understanding of yourself to truly nail your style. Knowing who you are and your purpose in life helps define your style.

▌PASSION

What do you love to do? Many of us take a long time to figure this out or procrastinate due to fear of failure. Once you find something you're passionate about, work on it every day, and this will start to define your personal style.

▌PROCESS

How do you do that thing you love? Process is one of the key elements for finding your style. Your individual processes help define your way of working and ultimately dictate the way you visually communicate. My sketch process has dictated my own style. I have leveraged that to communicate my ideas and am now known for my "process" and the way I communicate visually.

▌PATIENCE

The three key points above will only come to fruition if you give yourself time. Too many creatives don't give themselves the time needed to become what they want to become. We all have to fail, get up, fail, and get up again to understand what works and what doesn't.

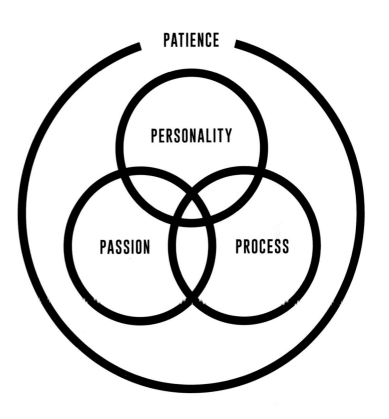

HABITS AND ROUTINE

Establishing a consistent and effective daily routine is truly the one thing I wish I learned earlier in life. I used to think, "I'm a free, awesome creative and I work how and when I want," but this quickly got me into a lot of poop mentally and created a negative impact on my productivity.

I'd draw into the early hours of the morning and pull all-nighters on the regular just to get stuff done. I'm not saying this is wrong, since I know circumstances and life in general sometimes knock us off our plans. But I've become a much more successful designer by sticking to good habits and a solid working routine.

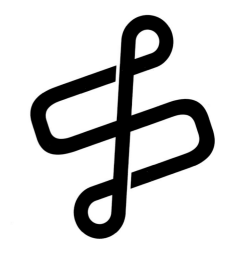

As with anything we do, there must be a process, and I know that if I want longevity within my industry and my creative brain to last, my routine is going to be a key component to making that happen. I try to keep my life pretty simple because it helps me find clarity.

The knock-on effect, or secondary effect, of keeping things simple has been huge for my development, both as a creative and as a tiny little chubby human. My day is broken down into easy chunks and looks like this:

* 6:00 a.m.: Wake up

* 6:30 a.m.: Read

* 7:15 a.m.: Walk the dog

* 8:00 a.m.: Head to the office and start work

* 6:00 p.m.: Leave the office

* 10:30 p.m.: Go to bed

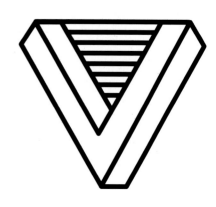

On the weekends, this routine changes—you know I like a little G&T—but the workweek always looks like this where the day belongs to my clients and the evening is mine. This schedule allows me to know what I should be doing at any time of the day, and more importantly, it lets me know when I can switch my brain on and when I can switch it off. Having the ability to do that is the biggest superpower you can possess as a creative and business owner.

Habits and routine tend to go hand in hand. For example, making coffee in the morning leads me into the next habit of heading to the office, etc. Habits can become a great trigger for your next move during the day, so creating a load of good habits can ultimately lead you to a productive routine. Those positive triggers help you stay on track for the day ahead.

Don't turn your life upside down tomorrow. As with anything, you should implement changes slowly to make them successful. Start with changing one thing and go from there. You can shower, change out of your pajamas and into work clothes every day, and exercise for at least half an hour. Adding tiny positive details to your day will, over time, help you be more relaxed and, in turn, more productive. We are creatures of habit, so make them good ones.

LITTLE TIP

A good routine helps eliminate creative block, so the sooner you can implement a solid routine into your day, the more productive and focused you'll become. I also like to tidy my office at the end of the day so it's ready for the following morning.

MINE	MY CLIENTS	MINE
06:00 TO 08:00	08:00 TO 18:00	18:00 TO 22:30

MINDSET MATTERS

The biggest killer of creativity is our inability to deal with our inner voices. I'm not sure if that makes any sense, but it does to me.

We are our own worst enemy when it comes to self-doubt and other negative emotions that many creatives tend to have swirling around in our brains. Do any of these sound familiar?

AM I GOOD ENOUGH?

ARE THEY BETTER THAN I AM?

WHY AM I BAD COMPARED TO THEM?

Whether you've been working for two weeks or twenty years, if you're a creative, I don't think these thoughts ever truly leave you. But you do eventually learn how to deal with them a lot better. Also, the older you get the less you care about what others think—in a positive way, obviously.

LITTLE TIP

Creativity is not a competition and comparing yourself to your peers is not good for the brain. We are all on different journeys and moving at different speeds, and that's okay. Remember why you started on this wonderful creative adventure and enjoy the process of getting better every day.

No magic pill exists for creating a more positive mindset. The best way to move toward a more positive mindset is to give yourself time. Don't think about how good you are now, think about how good you'll be in ten years' time if you keep going. As I've said before, all good designers started out as bad ones. But over time, and with a lot of effort, the designers who kept trying knew they'd get better. And you will too.

This is why I'm a big believer in creating good habits rather than setting loads of unattainable goals. Don't get me wrong—I know what I want to do, and who I want to be in the future. But rather than setting these as goals to achieve by a certain time, I'm setting up the right habits, knowing I'll attain my goals if I continue to work hard.

I like to remind myself daily that effort is free. It costs nothing to wake up every day and put in a good shift. I understand it's not always easy to remain positive in life, but you can still put in the effort even when you're not at the top of your game. If you don't show up for yourself, why would anyone else?

"

THE BIGGEST KILLER OF CREATIVITY IS OUR INABILITY TO DEAL WITH OUR INNER VOICES.

"

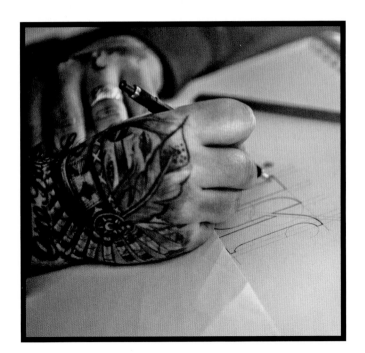

3 MY HONEST AND AUTHENTIC APPROACH TO LOGO DESIGN

Get that cup of tea ready and sharpen that pencil because this section is jam-packed with goodness you will need to underline. Everything I've learned over the last fifteen years is highlighted in this chapter to help you better understand how my mind and my creative process work.

I will forever be tweaking my personal process, since I know it's not perfect, but that's what we do as creatives. We should always be developing and refining. Knowing how other people work helps us reflect on the way we work; let's call it the circle of creativity.

This is a deep dive into the way I think and how my ideas come together. There is always a method to the madness, and I'm excited to share mine with you. Let's go!

WHY I DRAW

My passion for drawing started at a very early age, on a particular wall, and with a particular red crayon, but we won't go back there again—sorry again, Dad! I draw so much throughout my logo process and the reason why is very simple: I just love it. Give me one hundred hours in a sketchbook over one hundred hours on a computer any day. I feel free in a sketchbook—that blank piece of paper screams opportunity with every page flip. When you're excited every day, how can you not love what you do?

We're in the industry of selling ideas and telling stories. Drawing is such a powerful way to communicate, show progress, and visualize the power behind your thought process. The reason I get a lot of logo clients is not because of the final execution of the logo, but because I show the journey of its creation. Drawing gives you the ability to document every detail and communicate the reasoning behind your decision making.

We want our clients to form an emotional connection to the work we create. Throughout history humans have handcrafted tools and formed unique attachments to them. I want you to see the process of logo design as the same process. Showing handmade workings and progress on paper allows your clients to form that same unique bond.

Drawing has been proven to increase brain power, allowing us to enter a deep concentration for the task at hand and shut off the world around us. Check out the work by author and speaker Sunni Brown, whose research and TED Talk on the importance of doodling for problem solving is fascinating. Back to the client: looking at a designer's drawings and their process of idea generation makes it easier for clients to understand our ideas and easier for us to sell them.

What have you got to lose? Even spending ten to fifteen minutes at the beginning of a project sketching some ideas will help kick your brain into gear and give you something extra to share with your clients. Most importantly, it will bring your focus on the job at hand.

LITTLE TIP

The perception that drawing must be good is nonsense. See it as a process of formulating ideas. When you see drawing as a way of creating, rather than art, it becomes an extremely powerful asset to your process.

Keep a small notebook with you at all times. Instead of jumping on your phone and scrolling through social media, use that time to doodle your heart out, make notes, or scribble something on a piece of paper and color it. This helps you gain more pen control, which helps you get better at drawing.

Before I had a cell phone, circa 1995, I would sit at my desk and doodle for hours while chatting to my girlfriend at the time. I didn't know that I was training for my career today. The more time you put in, the better you'll get.

MY WEAPONS OF CHOICE (A.K.A. MY DRAWING TOOLS)

I've lost, broken, and used thousands of different types of pens and pencils—I even have a graveyard for the ones I don't use anymore, which is a box stored in a cupboard. I don't actually bury them in the garden.

As with any skill that develops over time, you learn to perform better with specific tools. Certain drawing tools feel more comfortable to me. Some people may say that spending $50 on a pencil is madness, but they may also be the same people who spend $50 a week on take-out coffee. At least my pencil makes me money.

You must prioritize what's important when it comes to investing in yourself. You may feel you can't afford a book or set of pens, but you can afford to buy a new pair of sneakers or computer game. Think about the equipment you're purchasing as an investment in the future.

LITTLE TIP

The equipment you use, especially for drawing, doesn't have to be anything special. You can use a tattered notebook and a half-chewed pencil. Buying the best equipment will not magically improve your skills, but putting in time and practice will.

Ultimately your tools can get better over time as you have the resources to invest in better equipment. When I started I used a standard pencil and my light box was a window. Your brain is more important than the tools you use.

MADE BY JAMES

BELOW IS A LIST OF ALL THE TOOLS I USE DAILY TO DRAW AND CONCEPTUALIZE MY IDEAS:

* **PENCIL:** My Rotring 800/0.5mm never leaves my side. I love the weight and the control it gives me when sketching. It just works great and never misses a beat.

* **PENS:** Molotow and Sakura Pigma Microns are two favorite brands of pens. Both are great to work with and leave a quality finish.

* **SKETCHBOOK:** I use an Artway A3 spiral sketchbook because the paper quality and weight are spot on for me. I have about sixty of these filled to the brim.

* **RULER:** Anyone who has seen me on YouTube or Instagram will know my love for Margaret, my little 6-inch stainless-steel ruler. She is a badass.

IF YOU'RE STARTING OUT, HERE ARE MY GENERAL RECOMMENDATIONS FOR TOOL SHOPPING:

* **PENCIL:** Regular drawing pencils are absolutely fine and I would go with an HB.

* **PENS:** Any fine liner pens will work great. I recommend getting a pack of three or five that have different nib sizes to cover all the necessary details you need for thicker outer lines and thinner detail lines.

* **SKETCHBOOK:** Most sketchbooks are portable, but they don't have to be. I would suggest having a notebook for details and then a sketchbook for the more detailed process drawings. The reason I like spiral-bound sketchbooks is because they open flat and I can also remove pages for my clients if they ask for the drawings.

* **RULER:** I like 6-inch rulers because they're easier to work with at the scale I am drawing at. I've always used a metal ruler because they tend to keep their edge better than the plastic ones.

SUNRISE

YELLOW

FROM CONGO FLAG.

... ANDREI
EXISTING LOGO
DEVELOP FREI.

NEGATIVE
SPACE

LittleTm

HOPE.

WORK OF
TYPE

POINTS RELATE TO
AFTER ALL THE
... PLE IN CONGO

INVERT LOGO TO
SEE IF IT'S BETTER.

sunris
sunris

THE LOGO PROCESS: AN OVERVIEW

Having a good working process is important to keep projects running smoothly, and that process will be helpful when projects are going the opposite way. I'm one of those weirdos who loves working with clients, but you will run into some crazies along the way (in all honesty, that makes it all a little more exciting for me). An effective process will be your best friend in the good times and the bad.

What do I mean by process? When it comes to logo design, I have a series of stages I go through to make logos for my clients. My job is to make the logo design process feel seamless, effective, and most importantly, fun for the client.

Remember that this is an exciting time for your client. This is the birth (or rebirth, if they're rebranding) of their idea. Don't make it a clunky and arduous process that's not enjoyable; they're entrusting you with their baby, so make sure you look after it. Whenever I create a logo, I treat it as if it's my own. I see myself as a part of the client's company, and communicating that starts to build a strong relationship of trust.

Having a well-defined process also makes your clients feel confident and makes them believe you know what you're doing and that you have control of the situation. Often a project goes belly up because you allow the client too much room to get involved. The lack of a process allows your client the ability to take charge of the project.

Clients hire you because they can't do the job themselves. Take control, be transparent about the way you work, and never stray from that. Being in control of the project gives us the freedom to create our best work.

LITTLE TIP

When setting a delivery date for a client, build in a time cushion. Just because you can do something in a day doesn't mean it should be delivered tomorrow. Giving yourself a buffer on projects gives you time to evaluate your decisions and sleep on your ideas. It will also give you a bit of wiggle room if life gets in the way.

CASCARA

KNOW YOUR INDUSTRY

It's easy to get confused by some of the terms that get thrown around in our creative niche. The importance of knowing who you are and what you do is key to defining your audience. We all start out as creatives and then slowly drill down into a specific area of expertise. Let's start at the beginning with a breakdown of some of the titles in our industry:

* **GRAPHIC DESIGNER:** Graphic designers generally have a pretty broad skill set and a firm knowledge of many design disciplines. They communicate the need of the client through super awesome visuals, whether through print or digital. Most graphic designers will have a pretty good understanding of Adobe programs such as Photoshop, Illustrator, and InDesign, or their equivalents that are not Adobe-based.

* **LOGO DESIGNER:** Logo design is a niche within the graphic design industry. A logo designer's main job is to create memorable designs for clients, which can be in the form of a symbol, type, or mark that helps identify their brand.

* **BRAND IDENTITY DESIGNER:** Let's call this logo designer plus. Brand identity designers create logos and then visualize them in a clear and clever way across a multitude of assets. They'll show how the logo is to be used across a number of materials, from business cards to signage and everything in between.

* **BRAND STRATEGIST:** Brand strategists are involved in the big picture. They help define the company's vision, goals, target audiences, and personality, among other key elements. Many brand strategists plan and execute the tasks at hand. They can get paid top dollar for their work, but that relates to the amount of time and effort needed to do their job.

I consider myself a logo designer and brand identity designer. I create logos and play a key role in rolling out the visual elements for my clients, such as packaging, business cards, and other promotional content. Knowing your place in the industry allows you to double down on your powers and effectively communicate your skills.

TYPE FACE
HELVETICA

FONT
HELVETICA

THE LOGO DESIGNER'S GLOSSARY

Below are some terms that are associated with our industry. Logo designers need to have an understanding of these.

LOGO: A visual that helps identify a company

MONOGRAM: A design that consists of two or more letters that are connected

LOGO MARK: An identifying symbol that represents a company

LOGOTYPE: A custom-designed word (usually the company's name)

BRANDING: The process of actively shaping a brand

BRAND: The way a company is perceived by those who interact with it

VECTOR: An easily scalable image

TYPOGRAPHY: The technique of playing with type

TYPEFACE: A family of fonts, such as Helvetica or Futura

FONT: A particular style within a typeface, such as bold or italic

BABYGIANT®
DESIGN CO.

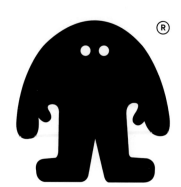

WORD MAPPING

Word mapping is a visual organization technique I learned in science class when I was about ten or eleven years old. Although I have zero recollection of the subject matter it was for, it's a very useful tool that I use today for creating ideas.

I use this technique for idea creation because it helps get the creative juices flowing and aligns me with the task at hand. Word mapping, in its simplest form, is a way of associating words with other words. Doing this helps me see a much bigger picture, which translates into more possibilities.

When I create these word maps, I'm not thinking about my answers too deeply, but I free-associate and write down the first word that comes into my head. I start with the key information from the brief, such as the company's name, its values, the industry it's part of, etc. I tend to begin with nine to twelve key points, or headers, to build a word map.

LITTLE TIP

When designing a logo, always ask yourself: Does this element need to be here? Simplicity is key, and if a design decision doesn't add to the overall idea, then remove it. Be clinical and don't diminish the other design elements for the sake of the one that's not working.

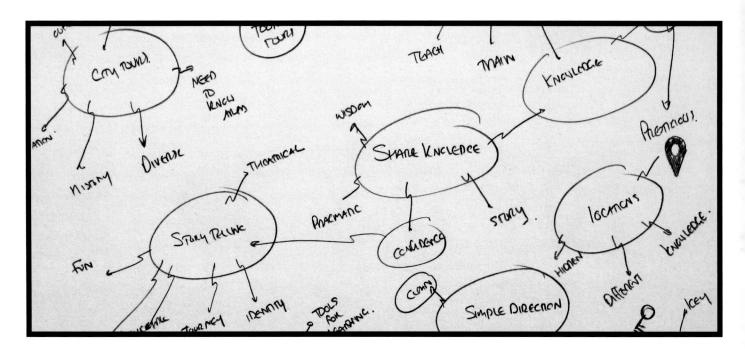

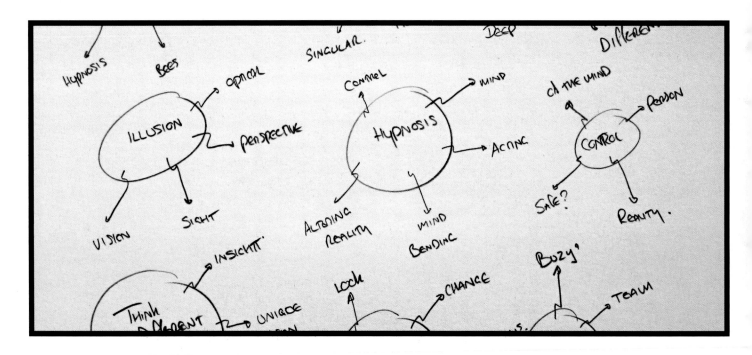

LITTLE TIP

Always design using the information that's in the brief; don't opt for cliché industry graphics. Just because your client is in real estate doesn't mean you have to include a house icon. Think deeper, think bigger—that's when unique designs start to happen.

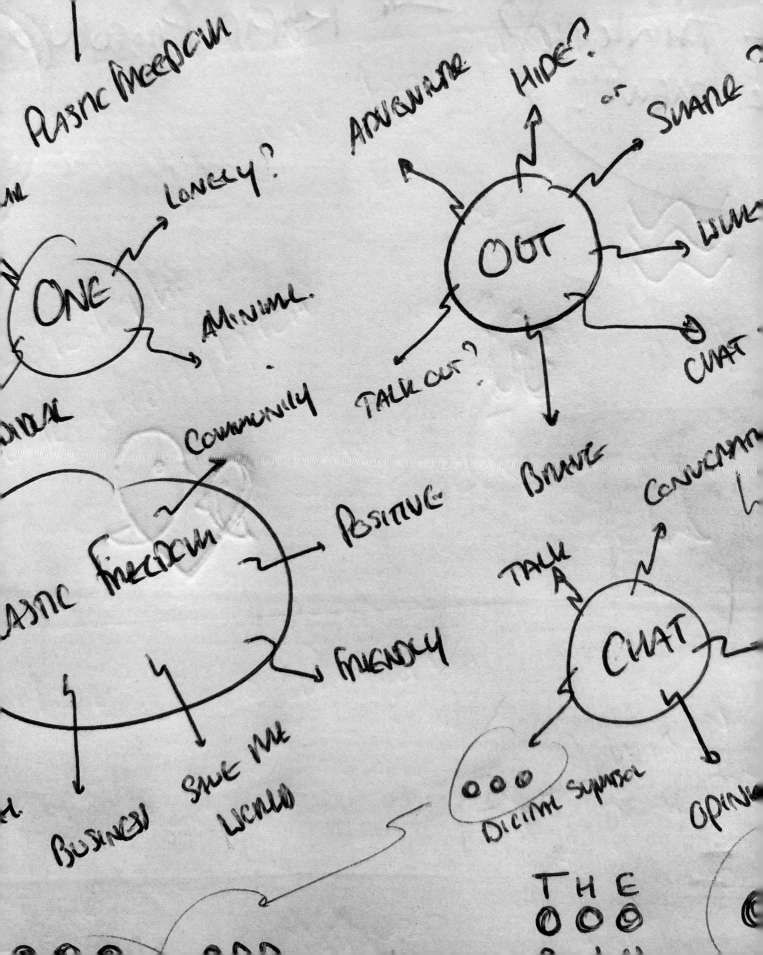

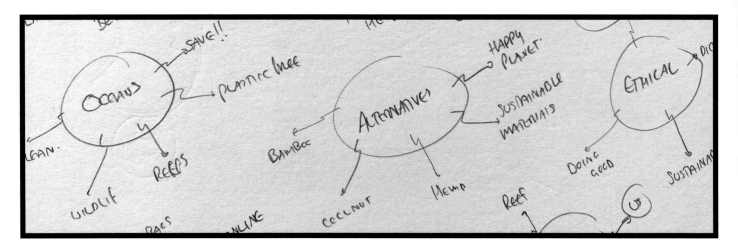

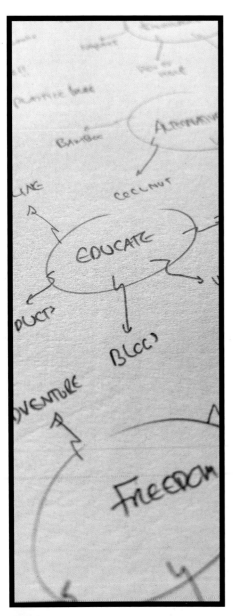

This process produces a picture and gets my mind thinking about the creative possibilities, rather than the obvious solutions, like a design for a coffee shop having the logo as a coffee bean. While I'm creating these word maps my mind begins to build a puzzle. I am asking myself how can I associate "X" in a certain way, or is there a way I can cleverly show "Y" without doing the obvious? For example, how can I associate the fact that there are three people within the company or how can I cleverly show that they are a family-based business? I'm creating a story and making sure my design decisions, however subtle, relate to the information I've been given.

I'll run through a few examples of how my mind works while word mapping, and you'll start to see how associating words with other words can open up options for creativity.

* **ENERGY:** speed, bright, electricity, movement, positive

* **PARTNERSHIP:** two, together, friends, marriage, even split

* **EDUCATE:** knowledge, sharing, learning, nurture, open

My options are pretty thin with the initial three words (energy, partnership, and educate), and it's difficult to think about the possibilities for creative direction with those three words alone. But with the added words that directly (or indirectly) relate to them, my options become plentiful.

I could have two shapes that come together (partnership), the colors could be bright (energy), and the two shapes I've chosen could be linked (sharing).

From this you can start to see the power of word mapping and how the technique can be a useful tool for idea creation. You don't have to be obvious with your concepts; often the subtle details make the difference between a good design and a great one.

RAPID PROTOTYPING

Rapid prototyping is an idea generator, a way of starting to change words and thoughts into loose concepts. This process allows you to quickly and effectively figure out viable directions for your logo and allows you to see what is and isn't worth exploring.

After completing the word mapping process, I have a plethora of possible directions to play with, and it's time to see what will work. I scan the word map for concepts and ideas and start to create visuals.

At this stage I'm beginning to home in on elements I can visualize into a logo, but I'm executing them very loosely and not trying to perfect any particular direction. I can't get absolutely every detail into a logo, so I typically choose three key elements to work with. Any more than that and the logo becomes a little too fussy and overcomplicated.

Anything goes during this phase—there are no wrong ideas, and I don't put any boundaries in place. I'm freely exploring directions that I believe I can make work. I'm not being too literal, and my main aim is to keep the design as minimal as possible so it will work in multiple sizes.

Your ability to think like no one else is your creative gift. Remember, your design doesn't have to be detailed to contain detail. You'll find there is a simple way to communicate your ideas. When it comes to logo design, simple, clean, and clever designs stand the test of time. Always think of the application of a logo: Where will it be used, and how will it be printed? These are key to your decisions and execution.

"

YOUR CREATIVE GIFT IS YOUR ABILITY TO THINK LIKE NO ONE ELSE.

"

Here is a glimpse into how my mind associates words with ideas. This process takes practice and a willingness to let go. Once you open your mind to thinking a little differently and taking more risks, options for creative concepts are abundant.

* **COMMUNITY:** can be visualized as the linking of more than one element, like a community coming together.

* **STRENGTH:** can be visualized as a solid presence. Bold shapes of color create balance and command attention.

* **HONESTY:** can be visualized as transparency, lending an honest and approachable feel.

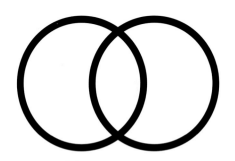

COMMUNITY

Linking Elements

STRENGTH

Filled Objects

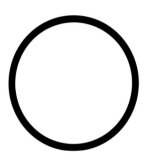

HONESTY

Transparent Shapes

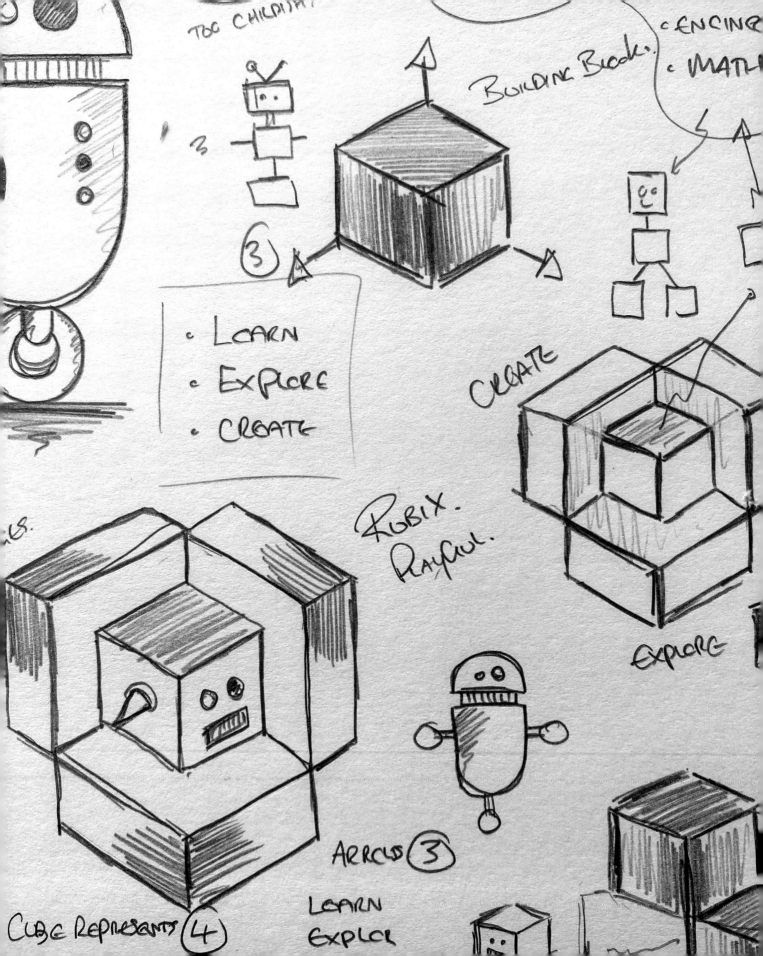

TOO CHILDISH?

BUILDING BLOCK.

° ENGINE
° MATH

- LEARN
- EXPLORE
- CREATE

③

CREATE

CREATE

RUBIX.
PLAYFUL.

EXPLORE

ARROWS ③

LEARN
EXPLORE

CUBE REPRESENTS ④

LOGO EXERCISE

▌ COMPANY: KARMA COLLECTIVE

I think most creatives learn best by doing. For this quick exercise, I created a fictitious company, Karma Collective, and chose six words that align with its values and company goals. Doodle for a few minutes to see what ideas you can come up with based on this information.

* **BACKGROUND:** Karma Collective is a group of designers that create illustrations, artwork, and brand identities for the plastic-free industries.

* **KEYWORDS:** honest, clean, vibrant, friendly, creative, community

Remember, you don't have to use all the keywords to create your logo. Choose two or three that resonate with you and have fun. Think creatively and see what's possible, using some of my ideas above. I did the same and I'll take you through my process and ideas on how I'd execute this project.

First, is there anything I could do with the letters *K* and *C*? Could I create a monogram or use the shape of the letters to depict other meaningful visuals? The company is all about saving the planet through the industry they work in, so could I depict the Earth in the designs?

After a few scribbles I realized I could break up the letter *K* into shapes that depict the letters *K* and *C*. Then, I thought about how to show the idea of a collective and a community. Replicating the shape and flipping it allowed me to create two elements coming together to create a whole. This represents the community coming together in a clean and subtle design. The real win is joining two semicircles to make a circle, which relates to the planet.

This cool little design has the company's name at the heart of the design, and I've kept the direction clean. The elements coming together shows a community aspect, and the circular shape celebrates the planet, which they're focused on every day.

DEFINING AND REDEFINING IDEAS

After word mapping and rapid prototyping, I make my final decision on the idea I want to run with and prepare the presentation for the client. I continue to refine the most powerful idea by asking myself more questions. If one of the answers is no, then I need to make some tweaks until all my answers are yes:

❋ DOES THE IDEA FIT THE BRIEF?

❋ DOES IT TELL THE CLIENT'S STORY?

❋ WILL IT WORK WHEN UTILIZED THROUGHOUT THEIR MATERIALS?

❋ IS THIS THE BEST I CAN DO?

WHEN IT'S TIME TO START OVER

Sometimes during this process, all of the questions get a "yes" answer, but once I get the design vectored up and ready to mock up for my clients, occasionally it loses its power. The idea is great, the sketch looks cool, but when I see the finished product I'm underwhelmed. This rarely occurs, but if it happens to you, don't worry. Take a deep breath, try to determine what's wrong, go back through the process, and hit it again. Don't waste time on something you know isn't going to work.

I'm still working in my sketchbook at this stage, finalizing a more accurate version of the design. Continuing to work in the sketchbook gives me the freedom to explore any tweaks. Should the corners be rounded? Should that line be thicker? Do the gaps need to be bigger? These changes could all be done in the computer, and further tweaks will be made there after I've vectorized my design. But I like leaving no stone unturned before heading to the computer. Any extra time spent working in the sketchbook saves me time working digitally.

Once I'm happy with the final sketch, I vectorize it in the computer. This is the process of taking a design and using computer software (such as Adobe Illustrator) to change it into a vector format, which allows you to scale the design without compromising the quality. Because of this capability, all logos should be created in vector format. To transfer my sketch, I simply take a photo of it on my smartphone and send it to the computer, where I import it into Illustrator.

Next comes the vectoring process, where you can refine the details and use further gridding techniques to make your design as accurate as possible. I use grids at the end of my projects to bring accuracy to my final design, making sure all the gaps (spaces between elements) are equal, and all my elements are aligned.

Setting up a specific grid before you have any ideas can restrict your creativity. Working to boundaries and rules stops you from exploring "outside the grid." I believe you should use a grid to help execute your final idea, not dictate your decision making from the get-go. When coming up

LITTLE TIP

Always take photos of each step of your design process. If you're working digitally, take some screenshots to record your process. We are in the game of content creation, so sharing aspects of the way you work on social media is a great way to give back to the creative community. You can also share the journey with your clients.

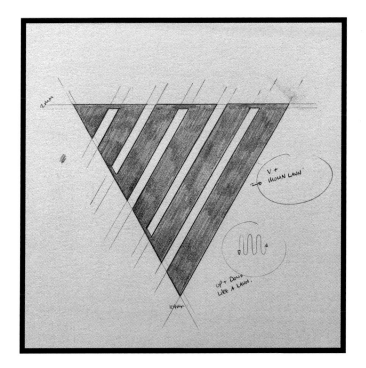

with our ideas, we want a blank canvas so there are no limits to what we can do. Remember that conforming to rules and setting strict boundaries can often have a negative effect on your creativity.

Once my design is ready, I create a series of mock-ups to show my client how I see the design working. I always show the design on visuals that pertain to its industry; for example, a brewery logo looks best on cans and bottles, and a design for a coffee roaster shines on bags and mugs. Showing your logo in context makes it easier for the client to understand its power, and you can sell it more easily. It's our job to show the whole story and how we see it working. A lot of clients won't have the vision to understand how it will work on a business card or a product they might have. Showing the logo successfully working across the assets they will use allows them to see the power of the design, rather than expecting the client to imagine what the logo could look like in a specific context. If the client can't see it working, they may feel it will never work. Allowing your clients to use their imagination is the worst thing you can do. As soon as you do that, you've lost them.

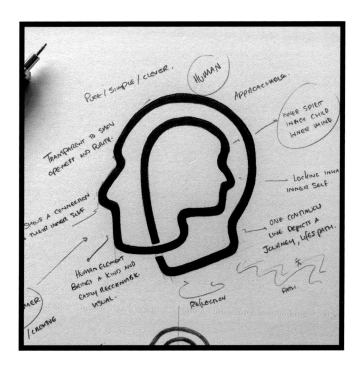

MBJ CHUNKY

PACK MY BOX WITH FIVE DOZEN LIQUOR JUGS

MBJ HANDWRITING

PACK MY BOX WITH FIVE DOZEN LIQUOR JUGS

MBJ DOODLES

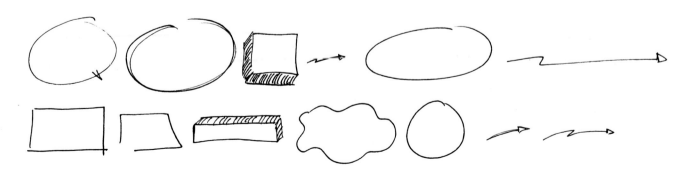

CREATING CUSTOM TYPE

When I began my career in logo design I never thought about type. I'd work hard at creating a cool symbol or monogram and then find a free font to go with it. Numerous fantastic font families are now readily available, which is awesome for designers, and there is absolutely no problem with buying or using a free one for your project.

I decided a while ago that this isn't the way I want to go with logo design because I don't want my creativity to stop at the symbol or logo mark. I love continuing the look and feel of a design into the type direction for my clients. I believe that occasionally the logo mark and logotype will need to work independently; sometimes the client will want to use one without the other, and this is why I like adding a little flavor to the type too. Even the smallest detail can make an ordinary type become extraordinary.

Adding a custom feel to the type allows me to continue the storytelling aspect of the design. Creating a fully customized direction (bespoke logo mark and type) gives my clients that feel-good factor, since all the elements of the logo have been considered and thought out. Creativity shouldn't stop at the logo mark. As designers we can keep that streak running all the way through to the type.

The best thing you can do with a custom type direction is to focus on one element. You can subtly hide multiple thoughts and layer your ideas when working with symbols. With logotype design, however, you want to keep it simple, especially when there is a logo mark involved—you don't want them wrestling for the viewer's attention.

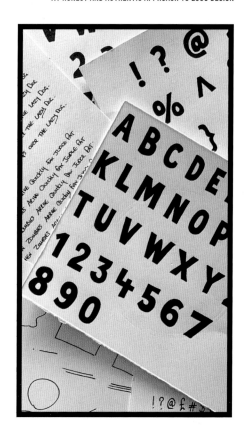

LITTLE TIP

Showing your client that your creativity is transferred into the type allows you to charge more for logo design and ultimately give your client a better offering. This practice can make you stand out among designers who leave the type alone.

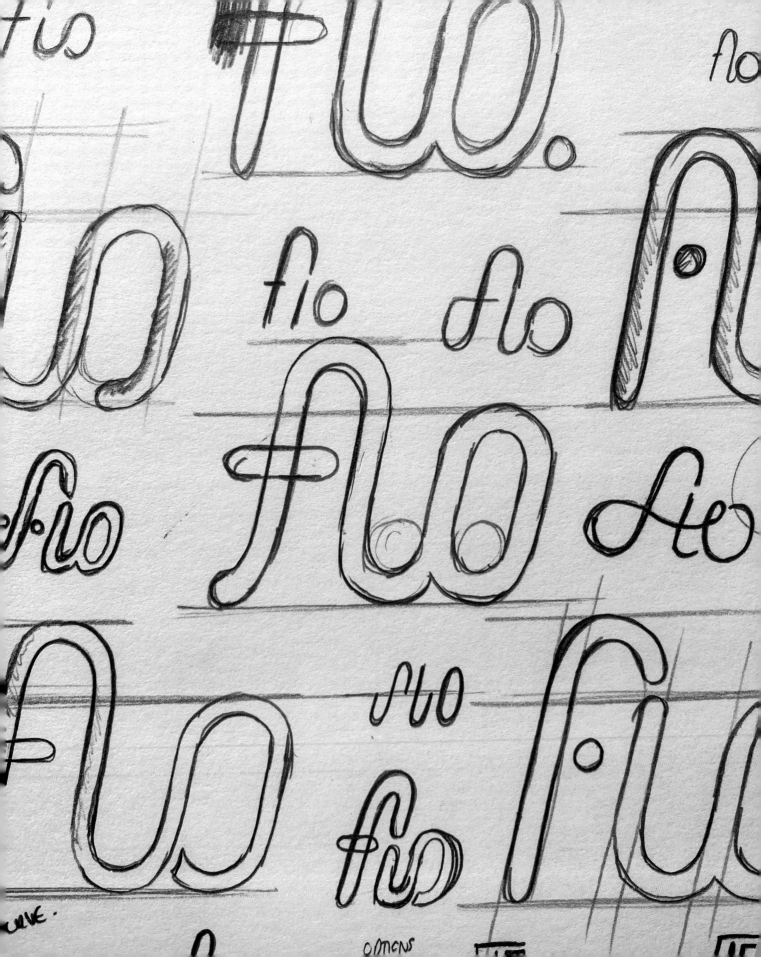

When I designed this Don Cuervo type I knew it was for a Mexican restaurant, so I want to add a little bit of that vibe into the type. Mexican lettering is known for its flare and the lettering often has little details added to the stems of the letters. I researched traditional Mexican lettering and added a little bit of that styling into my logotype.

I wanted to create a direction for the Weird Bear logotype that was memorable and complemented the name, so I did a play on the word "weird." Adding random curves and wobbly edges to the type and making all the letters not conform to the normal practices of alignment allowed me to create a custom type that aligned itself with the name and the client's vision for the company. Flipping letters and using the 3 as the letter *E*, representative of the founder's three children, adds personality and story to the design.

You can see from these examples the distinctiveness that custom type can bring to the overall identity of a logo. The next time you get a logo project, why not take all of that energy and add it to the custom type as well? Here are some ways you can practice creating bespoke type.

* **HAND-DRAWN:** Creating hand-drawn type is my favorite way to develop cool type directions for my clients, especially businesses that have organic and eco-friendly components. Hand-drawn edges add an approachable and ethical vibe to type. Work on individual letters or a whole name or word in your sketchbook, then take a picture of your work and create the vector files in Adobe Illustrator.

* **USE AN EXISTING FONT AS A BASE:** Find a font that you like, print out the name or word you want to work with, and draw over it using a light box. This allows you to add flair and cool quirks while not having to worry about layout and spacing. Try this using your name and creating five different variations. Use a copyright-free font if you're creating something for a client. If you're just practicing, use any font you like. You can add serifs, make it bolder, remove parts of the letters, have certain letters linking, etc. This exploration and playfulness with type can benefit future client work because you can start to add that flair to the real-world projects.

* **DESTROY AND REBUILD IN ADOBE ILLUSTRATOR:** As an alternative to drawing, find a free font online and play with it in Illustrator. Smash it apart, make the letters bolder, add angles, curve some parts, flip letters—destroy it and build it back up until it works for you. This is a great way to practice playing with type, and the results are always fun.

BUILDING BRAND IDENTITIES

A logo is just one part of a brand identity and, in the grand scheme of things, an even smaller part of the brand as a whole. As I mentioned earlier, a logo is a recognizable symbol, and the brand identity is a collection of assets to which the logo is applied.

I believe logo designers should also be brand identity designers. And, most people who call themselves logo designers are actually brand identity designers. If you have mocked up a logo on a business card, letterhead, or even a bit of signage, you are well on your way to being a brand identity designer.

The identity is what people see, and that can be colors, typography, packaging, print examples, and online elements that are part of web design, social media, and even video. The most important thing to bear in mind when creating powerful brand identities is consistency.

It's important for logo designers to practice brand identity and add it to their offering because we are storytellers. Imagine the logo being the title of the book and the brand identity being everything else. The logo may grab people's attention, like the title of a book, but the content keeps you engaged and talking about it. That's brand identity.

LITTLE TIP

I like to approach my presentations with what I call a six-four-two scenario: Six of my mock-ups are industry specific, four are for other relevant options such as business cards and general paper options, and two are outdoor options, such as signage, trade stands, and vehicles. This depends on the project, so alter yours accordingly.

Our job is to show clients the logo working *in situ*. As I mentioned previously, allowing clients to use their imagination leaves you with little control over the design. Building the identity around your logo design helps sell the concept you're presenting. As an added win, you'll show the client that you've thought about the relevant touch points. Here are some things to consider when creating a brand identity:

* **SHOW THE LOGO WORKING IN MULTIPLE SIZES:** A logo must work in multiple sizes in most circumstances because it will likely be used and viewed multiple ways and on different platforms, such as print, computer screens, mobile devices, etc. Be sure to ask where the logo will be featured and presented at the beginning of the project, and then prove that it works in those situations.

* **SHOW THE LOGO WORKING WITHIN THE SPECIFIC INDUSTRY:** Make sure there are a number of industry-specific mock-ups within your presentation. If the client is an apparel company, make sure you show the logo working in the right context for them: printed on T-shirts, embroidered onto hats, printed on bags for packaging, etc.

* **ADD YOUR OWN IDEAS:** Thinking above and beyond what the client has asked for is a great way to add value to your work. Think of clever and creative ways the logo could be used to help build the brand identity—can it be replicated to create a pattern? If the client mentions that one day the company hopes to have an app, show them the design that way. Anything you can do to help sell the idea is only going to help you.

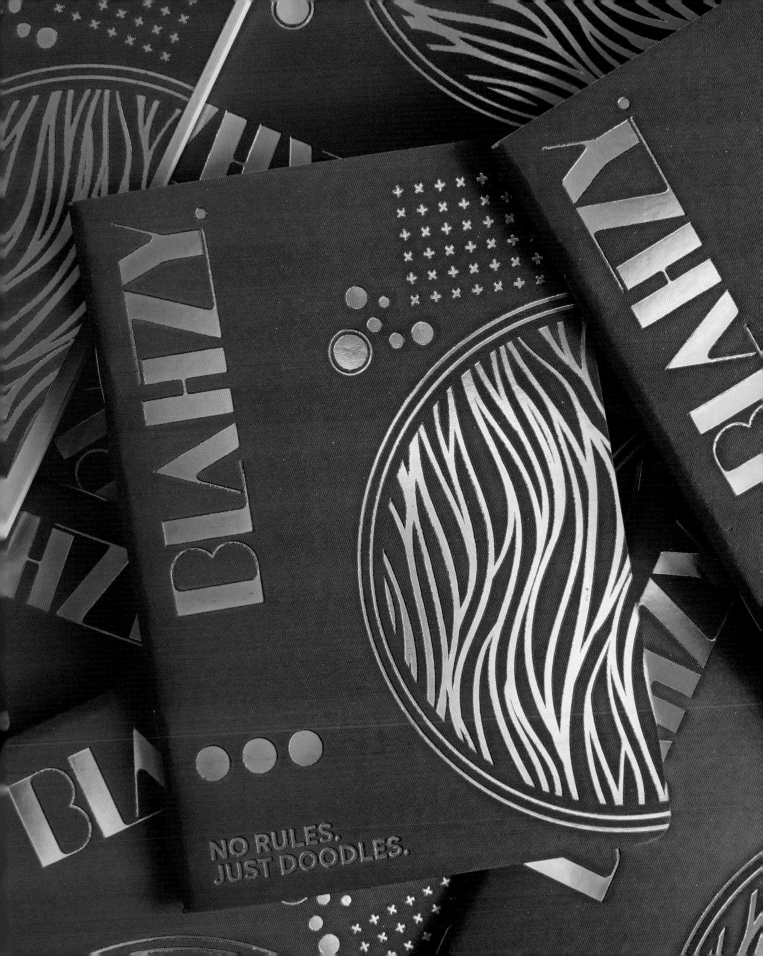

ONCE YOU HAVE THE DESIGNS READY TO SHARE WITH THE CLIENT YOU CAN PRESENT THEM IN A FEW WAYS:

* Attach them to an email with an explanation of your decision-making process
* Create a pdf of your designs and include text on your process
* Present your ideas via videoconference and talk through your thoughts

However you decide to share your ideas with the client, make sure you leave no stone unturned. Relate your ideas passionately and explain how you've made your decisions. Make the process enjoyable and sell your ideas with as much love as you put into creating them.

▎MY LOGO PROCESS TIPS

I've made many mistakes in my career, but I've learned from all of them.

On the following pages I'll share the way I've handled challenging situations that all designers face, and will face, over the course of their careers. Designers are open and caring to a fault and our passion for what we do is probably our biggest weakness. But to truly turn this hobby into a long and successful career we need to learn how to assert ourselves as professional businesspeople.

We need structure, and we need to be able to react to situations in positive ways so we can work effectively. How can we make money? What should we do when things go wrong? How can we grow into the creatives we want to be?

There must be a system in place for us to be able to express ourselves. How we handle our day-to-day business and interaction with our clients often gives us the clarity needed to be at our maximum creativity. So, hold on to your trucker hats, team—here's some advice and information that I'm sure will help you on your creative journey.

IDEAS FOR IDEAS

The techniques I've shown you have helped me create unique and memorable logos. Seeing the project as a whole and breaking it down into a series of related words allows me to explore every possibility, instead of being confined to a single idea, a set of boundaries, or the go-to industry standard.

The gift we possess is our ability to interpret things in different ways. Rather than going for the obvious, I like playing with subtlety and exploring the limits. We're taught that good design is obvious, but I think this phrase produces lazy creativity. Can't good design be well thought out, make people engaged, and still be effective?

Does an art supply logo need to have a paintbrush or pencil? Does a garden maintenance company have to have a lawnmower? Yes, that works for the industry, but does it really push the boundaries of creativity? The safe and obvious option may not always be the right one.

When I go through my idea generation process, I think of abstract ways to visualize certain elements. I create a logo for the brief, rather than creating a logo for the industry. I don't cloud my judgment by restricting myself to industry norms, and instead try to explore the feelings, words, and stories from an individual brief.

The brief and the human putting it together for you have a story behind them. Visualize that rather than the classic paradigm for any particular business. Adding personal details to a design can help your clients form deeper attachments to your work. For example, in the Vexquisit logo I added an animal because the CEO has a deep love for them. As you go through your process, don't think, how can I make this as obvious as possible? Instead, consider, how can I make this unique for my client?

The next time you come up with an idea, ask yourself, have I pushed the boundaries of this project brief? Have I explored more than the obvious options? Your answers will help you look at the design process with a more open mind.

LITTLE TIP

When working with a client, always ask for the company's history or the background of the people running it. This gives you great details for idea generation that can add unique elements to a logo.

THE IMPORTANCE OF COLLABORATION

Delegating work is not about losing control, but about gaining the freedom to be more effective.

Keeping your eye on the bottom line is important in the early days of any business—we have to do everything we can to stay afloat. When I was starting out, I was a web designer, illustrator, email marketer, idea generator, graphic designer, animator, administrator, accountant, and director—it's tiring just writing all of that.

This created a massive void in my productivity. I handled a huge number of things, but since I wasn't proficient in many of them, I lost money and squandered time. We can't do everything. This slippery slope can lead to burnout and depression, and also result in a massive waste of time, energy, and talent.

Understanding the power of delegation is the only way to make progress on your creative journey. I don't mean you should sit in a chair and bark orders at other people while taking zero responsibility for anything. Delegate in a way that gives you the opportunity to do what you do best. This allows others who excel at things you don't to become involved and lighten your load. To have longevity as a designer in a chosen field, you need to learn how to collaborate with others.

LITTLE TIP

Local colleges and universities are great places to find skilled young designers who need real-world experience. Contact the institution's internship program to see how you can participate.

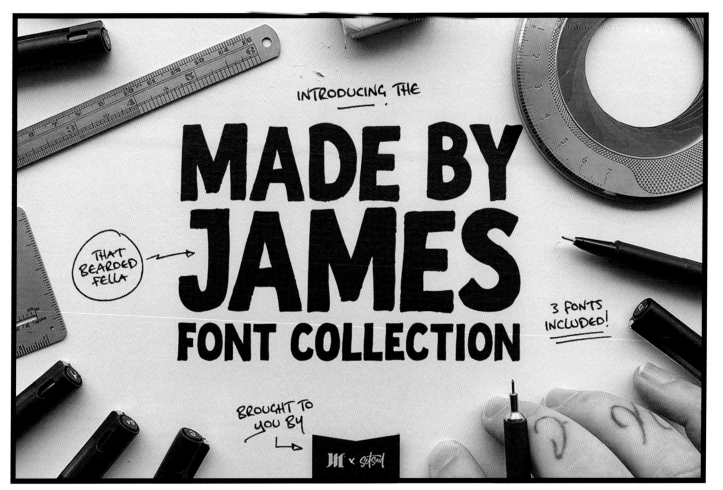

"

I GUARANTEE THE COST OF HIRING PART-TIME HELP TO ASSIST WITH ACCOUNTING OR DESIGN IS MUCH LESS EXPENSIVE THAN TAKING A FEW WEEKS OFF DUE TO BURNOUT. ASKING FOR HELP IS NOT A WEAKNESS—IT'S A SMART PROFESSIONAL CHOICE.

"

A Tour of My Studio - James
Martin - Made By James

2.1K views • 1 month ago

My Daily Logo Gear - Made
By James - Logo Life - EP#7

3K views • 3 months ago

18:21

Is Creative
Made By ~

1.9K views

17:02

2:31

ES MARTIN - LOGO LIFE
2 - MY LOGO PROCESS

s • 11 months ago

JAMES MARTIN - LOGO LIFE
- EP#1

8.7K views • 1 year ago

CREATIVE GROWTH

Everything seems perfect in this crazy social media world: idyllic holidays, beautiful plates of food, even (and scarily depressing) flawless selfies. I urge you to look at creativity in a different way. Imperfections are what make us and our work perfect. Striving for perfection prevents you from becoming a fantastic designer with an epic career.

Growth as a creative person is an individual journey, one you must embrace and be patient with. I've looked at other designers' work and thought, "Crappo, they are way better than I am." This is the classic imposter syndrome thought process that kills creativity. If you've ever doubted your skills, or thought you're not good enough, then welcome to being a creative.

Many of us were told growing up that being a perfectionist is important. That might be true for brain surgeons or rocket scientists, but people in creative fields? Not so much.

It's easy to forget how much we all have in common. Instead, we compare our abilities to draw, paint, or write, and think of them as the only barometers of success. We're all on the same path—some are at the beginning, some in the middle, and some at the end—but the path is the same. We want to be successful. Instead of creating barriers, why not harness this knowledge as fuel to create?

There is only one you on this planet, so show the world that person, including all your little quirks and nuances. Proudly put your work out into the world, whether it's finished or not. Trust me, it's better to be judged for trying than to judge yourself for not trying at all. Be brave.

The following are a few ways I keep myself motivated and driven to grow.

BE CONSISTENTLY, UNPREDICTABLY CONSISTENT

I like to keep myself guessing and my mind open to new things, but whatever I do it will always be based around my life and logo design.

BE CONSISTENTLY: Always be true to my mission to help people get better at logo design as well as share my honest thoughts and authentic self. I'm always sharing knowledge but in different ways to keep it fresh and interesting, and its "consistently" around logo design and creativity.

UNPREDICTABLY: Share my knowledge through drawing, video, and writing. This is unpredictable because people don't know what I am going to share next. They come to my feed to be inspired with an animation, a client project, a motivational carousel: I keep it changing and unpredictable.

CONSISTENT: Maintain my personal style and ways of communicating.The knowledge I share is consistently about creativity and logo design, which allows me to have fun, to continue to grow my mind and skills, as well to keep my following engaged.

KEEP ONE FOOT IN THE PRESENT AND ONE FOOT IN THE FUTURE

I learned this from Bob Iger, former executive chairman of the Walt Disney Company, and it's been a great way of growing personally and creatively.

PRESENT ME: Continue to offer my knowledge freely and build my company. Wake up, work hard, stay humble.

FUTURE ME: What can I do to help more people and be more accessible? What technology can I use to make my mission easier? How is the world moving, and where do I want to be ten years from now?

I REMEMBER THAT THERE ARE 1,000 PEOPLE BETTER I AM (WHICH THERE ARE)

The day I think I have this creative game all figured out is the day I hang up my trucker hat and put the pencils away. No one person is the best at anything, so this ideology helps me stay grounded and focused on the task at hand.

▌THE PROCESS OF ~~FAILURE~~ LEARNING

I landed my first design agency position in 2005. One of my tasks was to Photoshop a number of images for a local architectural firm, and then liaise with a framer to get the images beautifully mounted for the firm's new office walls. I spent a few weeks making sure the ten-plus images where correctly edited and the artwork was good enough to be printed. I took these to have them printed and framed, and the framer asked me several questions about a process I didn't understand. I nodded as he spoke so he wouldn't think I was clueless, which I was.

When I went to collect the finished artwork a few days later, the imagery was unmounted. This wasn't what the client asked for, the result of failing to correctly answer one of the framer's questions. Subsequently, all the images had to be reframed, and the extra work cost my boss a chunk of money.

Failure is such an important learning tool and helps us grow professionally and personally. Making mistakes is part of being human, but making the same mistakes repeatedly shows a lack of self-awareness. If you continue making the same mistakes you may need to reassess your learning process, your comprehension, and how you execute decisions.

"
FAILURE IS SUCH AN IMPORTANT LEARNING TOOL.
"

LITTLE TIP

Curiosity may have killed the cat, but it saved the creative. Never rely on inspiration from only one source or industry. The world is abundant with value, knowledge, and advice. Answers to your questions are out there, so go find them (P.S.: No cats were harmed in the making of this tip.). Seeking inspiration and learning from multiple sources is a massive contributor to learning.

"ENJOY THE PROCESS OF GETTING

  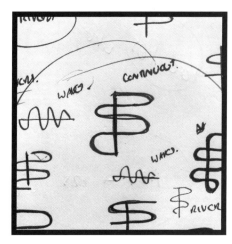

ALLOWING YOURSELF TO BE TERRIBLE

Allowing our creativity to blossom, making mistakes, doing bad work, and generally thinking we suck is important and part of the process, and shouldn't be missed.

When I was a young designer, I was bad at logo design and web design, my layouts were atrocious, my software skills were laughable, and I struggled to voice my ideas and opinions, as I always felt I was wrong. These feelings are common, but they didn't deter me from pursuing my dream of being a designer.

I knew from a young age that the creative industry was for me. I loved it. The thought of turning my hobby into a career was the most wonderful thing, but I knew it wouldn't happen overnight. I had to be patient, I had a lot to learn, and I needed to be persistent and practice daily to keep the dream alive. Becoming anything takes sacrifice, hard work, and patience. Patience is just as important as practice when it comes to being a successful creative.

If you've been in the industry for six months, don't compare yourself to someone who has a decade of experience. Don't rush and cut corners for quick gratification or to collect likes on Instagram. Remember why you started in the first place and put in every ounce of effort you can to make your dreams come true.

If you ever feel anxious or worried that you're not good enough, shift your focus. Take a step back and focus on the things you have achieved instead of the things you haven't. Your creative career will likely span more than forty years, so stop judging yourself after one or two.

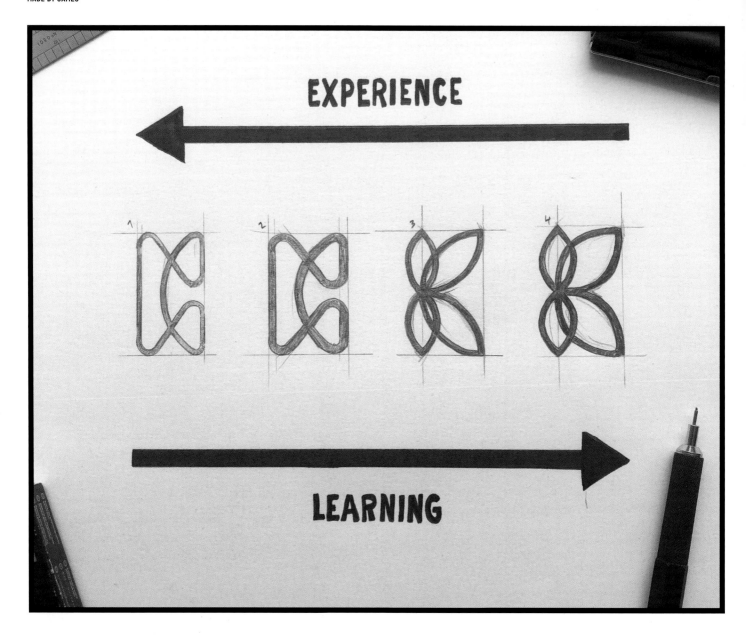

> ## "
> # I NOW HAVE ZERO PRESSURE TO BE RIGHT ALL THE TIME.
> "

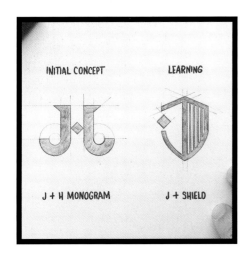

REPLACE THE WORD *FAILURE* WITH *EXPERIENCE*

I used to get down on myself—a lot. As creators, we all have an emotional attachment to our work, and that's an awesome thing. We've put our heart and soul into it.

As I've progressed in the industry, I realize that feedback, both positive and negative, is part of the creative process. Often the work we create that doesn't make the cut is not bad at all, it was just not right for the client.

This mindset shift has helped me be more in control of the work I create. I no longer see rejected ideas as a slap in the face; they're part of the process that allows me to think about the possibilities for new ideas. I get the chance to do something even better for the client.

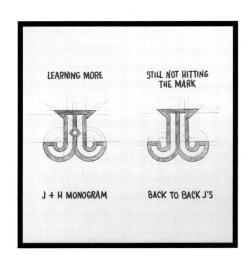

Producing work that doesn't make the cut isn't a failure, but a way of learning and gaining experience. This thinking has given me so much more headspace when it comes to creating ideas. I now have zero pressure to be right all the time.

For example, the drawings on this page are from a recent logo project I did for a company called Jackhammer and the concepts I developed to reach the final design. This clothing company that specializes in men's workwear and apparel was started in 2011 by four college buddies, all of whom had an engineering background and a love for fashion.

I thought the initial concept I presented to the company was cool, and the client liked it, but it wasn't working for them. There was too much emphasis on the letter *H* being added to the logo—it didn't work, especially since Jackhammer is one word. After a few more tweaks and going back to the brief, I realized I hadn't integrated a key piece of information: the company was started by four friends. I altered the design so the final iteration depicted four interlocking J shapes. The logo celebrated them and what they came together to create. Without being wrong a few times I would never have gotten to this final design.

The key to becoming a successful designer is remaining passionate about all the work you do while accepting the possibility that not everything you'll create will be right. Every design you do won't be a home run—and if they were, you'd get bored pretty quickly. Adopting simple word changes can help this new way of thinking take root in your mind.

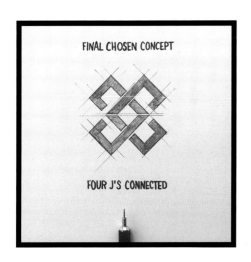

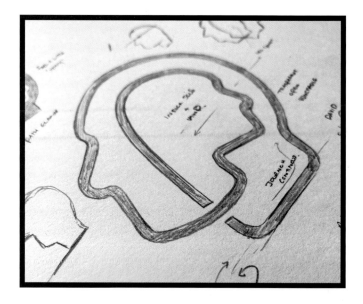

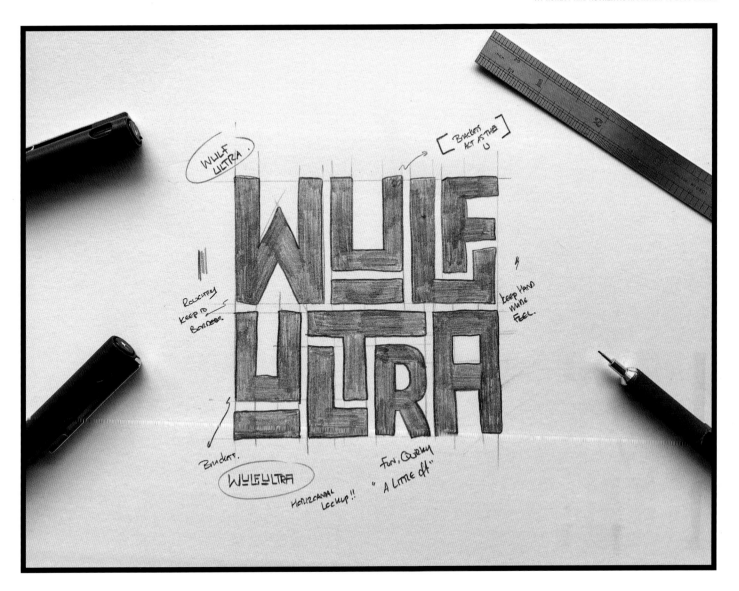

NEGATIVE THINKING: I HAVE TO DO ANOTHER LOGO.
POSITIVE THINKING: I GET TO DO ANOTHER LOGO.

WHICH DESIGNER ARE YOU?

ILLUSTRATIVE + TRIBAL
FEEL is ON POINT CUR
BRAND.

RESEMBLES
FACE + PARTNER

DOUBLE UP LINE
AND ADD COL

4 CIRC
COMING
EYE —
THE [

IN THE ZONE"

HARDWARE
FOR BALTIC
PRISE

4 LINES of
WARPAINT"

FUN / FRESH / ILLUSTRAT

KEEP TYPE

SYMMETRY.

THE ABILITY TO COMMUNICATE

Cool Approachable

- IMAGE
- TEXT
- IMAGE
- AUDIO

£3650

£2737.50

850
+ 2800

WHAT IS SOMEONE
IS OVER LOOKED

MASTER P

NO LIMIT RECORDS

SIMPLE BUT CLEAN

DIRECTOR

PACKING

- MODERN
- PIONEERING
- NOT TOO CORPORATE
- TRADITIONAL vs NEW

- CONVERSION

3 LINES PATTERN
TEXT IMAGE AUDIO

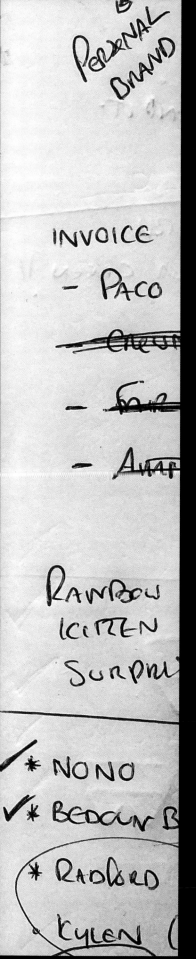

4 WORKING WITH CLIENTS

Clients are the bread and butter of any career-focused designer. Without them we can't build confidence in our work, we don't get paid, and we can't benefit from being referred to their friends and business colleagues. I find that client referrals are the easiest way to build a solid and trusted client base and create huge reach for your work.

In this chapter I dive into the process of client control and offer advice on how to handle specific situations you may encounter. As creatives, we need to be in control of the process, otherwise things can go south quickly. The good news is that the vast majority of clients you'll work with will be fantastic. Some may be a little difficult, but 1 percent will be unbearable.

I love working with clients and know that they'll be a big part of my journey, even when my hair starts to go silver and my back starts to ache a little more.

PROTECT THE ASSET: YOU

I once had a client reach out to me and tell me that I was "the only person who could bring his vision to life." Foolishly I took this compliment and battled away at his design. There were so many red flags I chose to ignore (the client saying "I'll know it when I see it" was one of them), but I carried on regardless. After many iterations that all matched his extremely loose brief, he said that I "wasn't the designer he thought I was" and started to attack me personally because I couldn't "read his mind."

For a very long time I never used to have any sort or formal contract in place and luckily it never bit me in the bum too bad. All it takes is one bad client to ruin a perfectly good day. The knock-on effect that a challenging client can have on your other projects, and your mindset, can be very damaging and counterproductive.

When working with a client there are a couple of ways you can protect yourself, and it's up to you how you want to roll with it. I recommend having at least one of these protections in place, since it will give you the peace of mind needed to do your very best work. On the rare occasion the project goes south, you'll be protected.

LITTLE TIP

If you have a bad feeling about a project, or about the person or people running that project, do not get involved. You have those feelings for a reason, and you have to trust your gut. Don't make a rash decision, though—ask if you can get back to them in 24 hours, and then make the right call for you.

GET A DEPOSIT

The standard working arrangement for designers is to request 50 percent up front and the remainder on completion of the job. No matter what process you want to follow, make sure you receive the final payment before sending the final logo files.

STATEMENT OF WORK (S.O.W.)

This is a document that describes the work requirements for a specific project along with its expectations. This defines the project timelines, deliverables, and working terms and conditions, and it should be signed by the client.

I include both of these practices in my process, and they provide both me and the client with clarity on the project. For the deposit, I ask for 75 percent up front and the rest on completion due to my specific process, which I'll explain in more detail over the following pages.

This is an ample amount of protection for a logo designer. You can go crazy and get big contracts written up if you feel that's a direction you want to take, but I think that's a little overkill. If you want to draw up legal documents, make sure you seek proper legal advice and not just grab information off the internet.

Having your working terms and conditions available on your website is another good practice. When I send invoices, I include a link to the terms and conditions on my site.

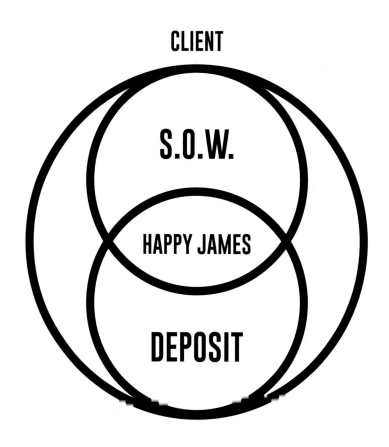

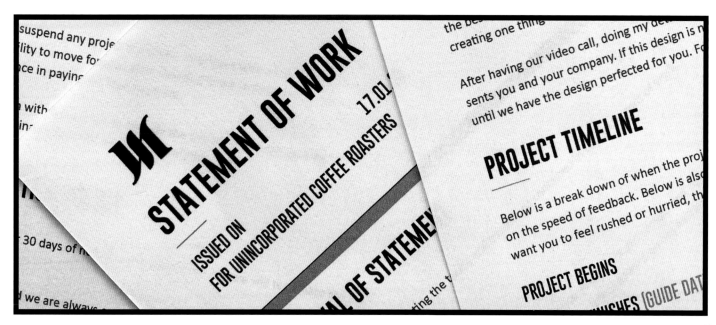

" YOUR EARS ARE MORE IMPORTANT THAN YOUR MOUTH. "

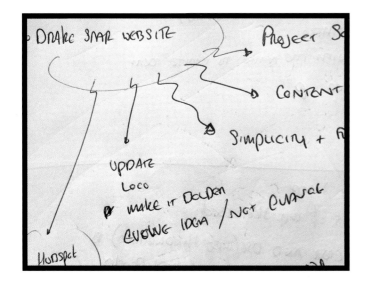

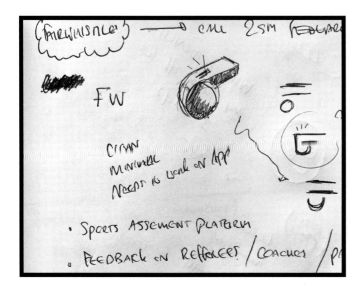

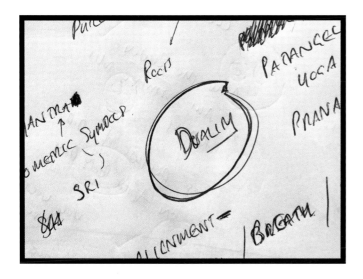

THE DISCOVERY CALL

I always find the term "discovery call" hilarious, since it makes me feel like I'm going on some sort of wild expedition or even flying to the moon, when all I'm doing is jumping on a phone call. But we creatives love to make things sound cooler than they are.

The discovery call is a very valuable part of the process, and the part that sets the tone for everything to come. I love jumping on a videoconference call with my clients because I like chatting to the people I work with, and I can start to gauge their personality and body language when they talk about the project. I'm able to read their reactions to my questions, and I can get a sense of their character and passion for the project.

Before the call is scheduled I always ask my clients to provide two things:

* **A MOOD BOARD:** In simple terms, this is a visual presentation consisting of images that serve as inspiration for the project. This can be sent via email, or most often I'm sent a Pinterest board.

* **A DESIGN BRIEF:** This is a document that details the parameters of the project and can include information such as the company's name, a description of the business, the company's values, its target markets, and any other information that tells me about the entire company. (See more about clients and design briefs on page 129.)

This information allows me to have prior knowledge about the company from the people who run it. Since they've supplied these assets, I know that everything I'm reading and looking at is accurate, and nothing has been miscommunicated.

LITTLE TIP

Your ears are more important than your mouth, so letting your client talk you through their thoughts and ideas is important. Don't be one of those designers who constantly butts in. You can get so much information by listening intently.

This process also reduces the guesswork that a Stylescape can sometimes create. A Stylescape is a design tool that communicates and guides the visual language of a project and is usually put together by the designer, not the client.

Before the call I have a good idea of what the company does, what makes them different, and what type of aesthetic they prefer. This is all fantastic information that we can discuss. I let the client lead the conversation on the call and give them the opportunity to talk me through their brief and mood board, and I let them know I'll ask questions along the way, allowing me the opportunity to listen clearly to what they're saying.

During the discovery call, I also talk the client through my entire process. This is a great time to be transparent about the way you work, which is key. You're emphasizing again that you are in control of the process, and always remind them that if they have a design problem, you're here to find the solution.

Ninety percent of your clients will be positive and happy there is a process, and they'll be more than happy to run with it. The other 10 percent may need a bit more convincing—but if they don't like your process, return their deposit and wish them the best of luck. This is a true red flag that indicates they want to be in control, and the project will go sideways quickly. Trust me, I've been there.

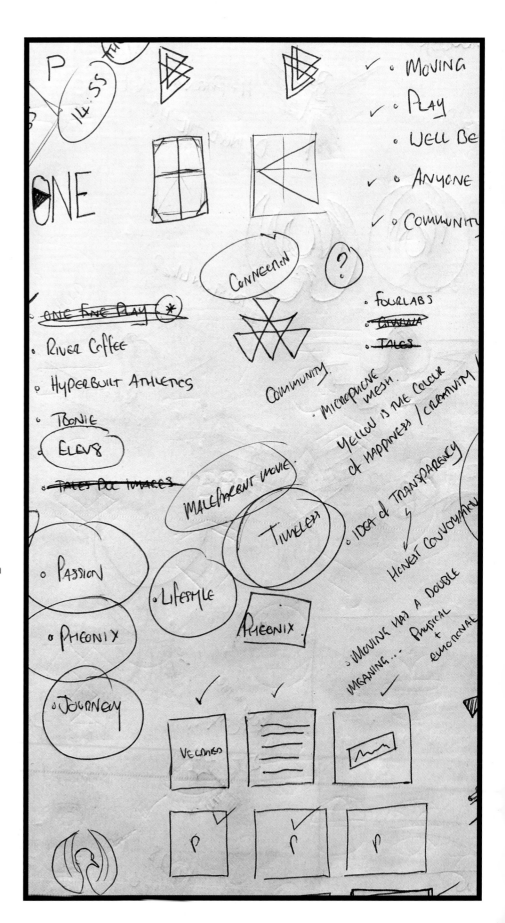

WHAT IF THE CLIENT DOESN'T PROVIDE A DESIGN BRIEF?

I get asked this question a lot, so it's worth elaborating about this. I've been approached a few times by clients who not only don't have a brief, but they also don't know what a brief is. That's absolutely fine—we have to remember that the rest of the world may not know everything we know.

A designer can help clients produce a brief. By asking the right questions we'll get the right answers, and all this information will help us create serious coolness. Here are some questions you can use to spark the conversation:

- What is the name of your company?
- How long have you been in the industry?
- What are the values and core beliefs of your business?
- What makes you different from your competitors?
- Why is this a good time to be in your industry?
- Where did your idea come from?
- Where and how will your logo be used?
- What creative assets need to be created?

Asking questions like these can help you obtain the information you'll need to create a new logo and any other assets they may need from you. The more information you have, the more ideas you can create.

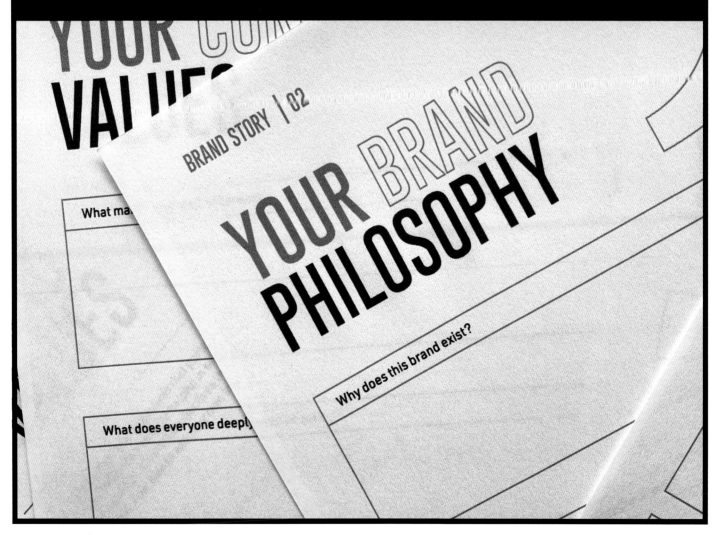

"
YOU NEED TO SAVE YOUR CREATIVE POWERS FOR THE RIGHT PEOPLE.
"

BEING IN CONTROL AT ALL TIMES

The most important thing to remember when working with clients is that _they_ have hired _you_.

You're the expert in this field of work, and you should take the reins and be in control of the process. The primary reason for a job going wrong is often because the designer isn't in full control of the project. Putting the blame on the client is easy, but you have likely allowed the client to take control of the process.

Your process and the decision to be transparent about it are the two most important assets you have at the beginning of any project—apart from your beautiful, creative brain. Being open and honest about the way you work is the catalyst for being in control. Lay out the foundations and process of how you work from the beginning, whether you communicate via email, phone, or video conference. Don't waste time communicating back and forth with the client before discussing these key elements:

THE PRICE: When a client reaches out to me for a logo design, I first let them know my pricing structure. By doing this I avoid wasting time on people who don't have the right budget.

MY PROCESS: I explain my logo creation process so there is no ambiguity about how I come up with ideas.

TIMELINES: I always let the client know when I'll start to work on the project and how long it will take. This stops any "I need it tomorrow" nonsense. Being in control of deadlines allows you to work efficiently and, more importantly, avoid burnout.

LITTLE TIP

Build in extra time to your delivery schedule for every project. You need time to reflect on your decisions, and you also need a buffer for unexpected events. Don't put unnecessary pressure on the process. If a job takes two days, tell the client you'll deliver it in a week. Give yourself time to breathe.

Some people won't like your approach and will want you to work a certain way or stray from your process. You have the power to make one of two moves:

1. Reassert your control by gently reminding the client that they hired you for a logo design because they like your work, which was created by the process you've described. Tell them that you do your best work if you follow that process.

2. If they're not willing to accept your process, that's a huge red flag. At this stage I let the client know I'm not the right person for the project and suggest they find another designer who's willing to work in the manner they prefer.

This may sound a little "It's my way or the highway," but to grow as a creative you need to save your creative powers for the right people. If they don't trust you to do your job, then wait for the people who do.

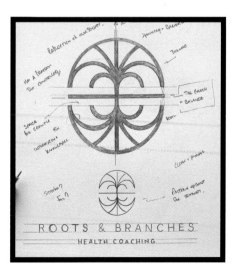

THE IMPORTANCE OF LANGUAGE

Language is an underestimated asset to a designer and can mean the difference between a winning or losing design concept. Using the right language when communicating can positively reinforce your message and validate your decision making.

Take this statement, for example:

> ## " I ABSOLUTELY LOVE THIS LOGO DIRECTION. I THINK IT WILL WORK FANTASTICALLY FOR YOU AND YOUR BRAND."

At first glance you may think there's nothing wrong—the words sound positive, energetic, and convey a positive thought process. Now, read this version:

> ## " I ABSOLUTELY LOVE THIS LOGO DIRECTION. IT WILL WORK FANTASTICALLY FOR YOU AND YOUR BRAND."

Saying "I think" when selling an idea to a client implies that you're questioning yourself. The words may seem harmless and conversational, but they could be the reason your design doesn't make the cut. As soon as you say "I think," you allow the client to also doubt your concept. In this example, the statement "I think" could be changed to "I know." This creates a positive reinforcement of your point and shows confidence.

The next time you create an email or document where you're selling a direction, pitching an idea, or persuading a client to work with you, make sure the language you use doesn't imply you're second-guessing yourself. I still check my correspondence all the time, as that language still sneaks into conversations from time to time.

LITTLE TIP

I'm seriously bad at spelling, so I read my emails a few times before sending them. This gives me a chance to check the grammar and spelling, and I can also remove any semi-positive or negative phrasing that could give a client less confidence in my ability. Clear correspondence that's free of errors allows you to come across as diligent and professional.

ECODODO

PRICING YOUR WORK

People have always struggled with appropriately pricing their work and have had to deal with the constant noise about the subject. Remember that the information you read is based on another person's experiences—they figured out what worked for them from experience and probably by getting it wrong most of the time. I know that's how I learned.

So many factors are involved when it comes to figuring out how to price work, including work process, the target market, overhead costs, experience, and deliverables, just to name a few.

This is why there's no one-size-fits-all scenario when it comes to pricing. The process involves constant trial and error and knowing how to use your knowledge to your advantage.

Being slightly older and a little wiser on the subject than I was when I started, I better understand how the industry works. I have a good grasp of what my target market is willing to pay, and just as importantly, what I'm comfortable earning.

Nailing down your value proposition as a creative is a massive contributor to figuring out pricing. If you don't know your professional skills and what services you offer, what makes you unique, and who your client base is, how on earth can you create a solid pricing structure?

These three questions can help you determine your value:

1. **What service or services do you provide to your clients?**

2. **What markets and industries do you cater to?**

3. **What makes you different from the competition, or what is your unique selling point?**

Research other companies online and find their value propositions. This will help you gauge the power of this exercise. This will also help you figure out your pricing and give you a reliable guide for your career. You can then establish your personal mission or create a mission statement. Here is mine:

MY MISSION IS TO PROVIDE MY CLIENTS WITH ICONIC AND MEMORABLE IDENTITY SOLUTIONS THAT THEY CAN STAND BEHIND TODAY, USE TO REACH THEIR GOALS, AND HELP GUIDE THEM IN THE FUTURE.

Once you know your value and mission you can begin to understand the best way to accurately gauge your price point for the creative services you provide.

Your process is the biggest factor in pricing a logo. I have the same process regardless of the client—I know how long it takes me to read a brief, do the word mapping, come up with ideas, and execute a cool design. Knowing my process well allows me to understand my timeline so I can accurately price jobs.

Here is a simple pricing formula that worked for me when I started out:

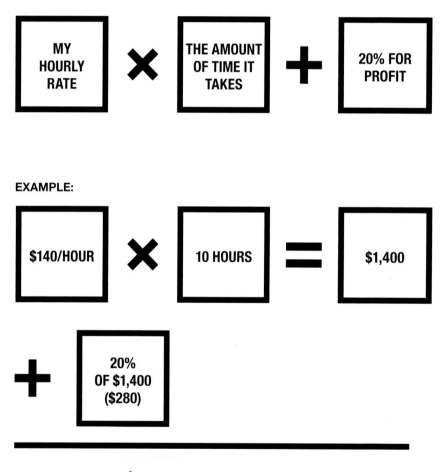

| MY HOURLY RATE | ✕ | THE AMOUNT OF TIME IT TAKES | + | 20% FOR PROFIT |

EXAMPLE:

$140/HOUR ✕ 10 HOURS = $1,400

+ 20% OF $1,400 ($280)

▎TOTAL = $1,680

"THE BIGGEST KILLER OF SUCCESS IS GREED."

Pricing isn't difficult when you understand that the key fundamentals are time and process. You don't need complicated formulas; you just need to understand simple math. Over time, and with the right experience, you can move into a more value-based scenario for pricing. This includes variables such as your experience, the advantages you bring, and the value your work brings to the client and their product.

Here's a good example of this: Imagine the cost of a sketchbook, a pencil, and a pen—not a huge amount of money. Imagine Banksy creating art with those materials. Now it would be worth a small fortune.

Banksy's name, experience, and other factors bring huge value to his work. In time, you'll also gain clout in your industry, but you have to start somewhere. Keeping it simple in the beginning will bring clarity.

Always remember that the biggest killer of success is greed. When the right project comes along I'm always open to a bit of wiggle room in pricing. I may make a little less profit on a project, but I'll have an epic piece of work out in the world that will bring me more work. Knowing your worth is important, but as a creative, recognizing opportunities and thinking about the long game are the real skills.

Understanding the time it takes to complete certain tasks is important. As the saying goes, time is money. Logging your time on a project allows you to understand your efficiency and effectiveness. Also, be aware of the daily costs to run your business, such as rent, supplies, insurance, equipment, electricity, maintenance, etc. These should be factored into your pricing as well.

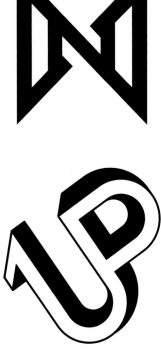

THE VALUE OF RUSH FEES

We've all been there—we start chatting with a client about a new project, explain the process, get to the part of the conversation about timelines, and they say they need the work finished for a conference they're attending the following week. (I'm always amazed how some of these people succeed in business; this disorganized work style must be super stressful for their colleagues and the people around them.)

I typically suggest they find another designer, since I don't need the hassle and the project usually doesn't excite me enough to get involved. But sometimes a supercool human comes along with a supercool project, and I need to make it happen. This is where I like to incorporate rush fees.

A rush fee is an amount of money added to a project's regular price that allows it to become your priority. If a client needs me to drop everything to get their work done in an unreasonable amount of time, I double my fees. The extra amount lets me accept working at unusual times, put in longer hours, and feel the effort is worth my while for a short period of time. Don't mistake greed for savvy business decisions.

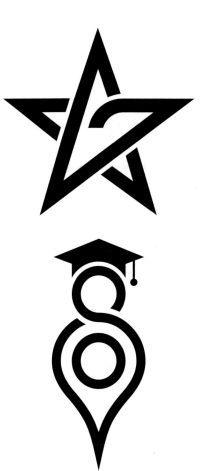

DECLAN SHIELDS

RACING

DECLAN SHIELDS

RACING

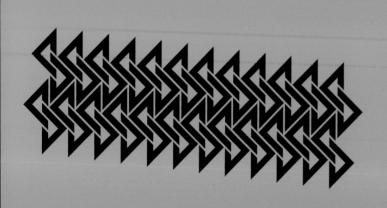

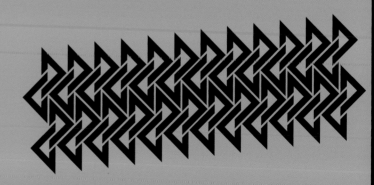

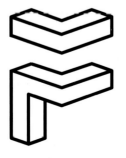

▌WHAT HAPPENS WHEN THINGS GO WRONG

No matter how much you prepare, there will always be a random moment when a random project goes randomly wrong. That's life, and sometimes stuff doesn't go the way you expect it to.

I'm sure you've been in a situation where everything is going well, and the client sounds satisfied and happy so far. Then—whammo! All of the toys are chucked out of the pram and the world seems to implode. You're left wondering what on earth just happened.

Everyone who can relate to this, raise your hand.

Often the implosion has nothing to do with logo design—it's just life. You never know what's going on in the background. Sometimes aspects of people's lives affect their work, and this can impact their mood, behavior, reactions, and judgment.

Remaining calm and not overreacting are the best things to do in this situation. I've done the opposite and achieved absolutely nothing, apart from creating headaches, anxiety, and lack of sleep due to worry. This is where your process becomes your friend. If you have the deposit and statement of work sorted, then you are still in control. You just need to fix the situation.

If a client isn't happy with your design direction, then this is a great time to ask some questions. Focus—don't get drawn into a he said/she said scenario. Work with the facts and communicate clearly. You might say something like this:

I CAN UNDERSTAND YOUR FRUSTRATION, BARRY, BUT REMEMBER THAT EVERYTHING IS FIXABLE. WHAT WE NEED TO DO IS FOCUS ON WHAT ELEMENTS YOU LIKE AND DON'T LIKE. THIS WILL ALLOW ME TO DEVELOP MY IDEAS.

"

"REMAIN POLITE AND PROFESSIONAL, AND REMEMBER THAT THINGS AREN'T AS BAD AS THEY SEEM IN THE MOMENT."

If you and the client aren't seeing eye to eye on a design direction, then jump on another call and face the challenge. Run the client back through their brief and mood board and ask why they feel the design doesn't match their vision.

Open and honest conversations with your client are important, even when you feel the client is wrong. Remain polite and professional and remember that things aren't as bad as they seem in the moment. Also, be open to the possibility that you may be the one in the wrong. Ask yourself what you may have missed, what you could have done better, and how you can resolve the problem.

The next time you're in a situation where things are not going according to plan, stop, breathe, and get on a call with your client. Realign your brain and facilitate an open discussion on how you both can get this project over the line. Most issues can be fixed with honest conversations.

LITTLE TIP

Never email your clients first thing in the morning if they've contacted you about a problem. Allow your brain to wake up, then grab a coffee and read for 20 minutes or go for a walk. Holding back an impulsive answer is always a good idea, especially when you're not awake enough to make a good judgment call. Read the email properly and then breathe. Now you're ready to communicate efficiently.

HOW TO DEAL WITH NEGATIVE CLIENTS

To this day I have the odd client who doesn't like the work I create for them, and that's fine. As long as they offer constructive feedback that helps me with my development process, I'm actually excited to continue working on the project. When this happens, my mind goes straight into competition mode with myself and I want to create something even better for them.

Another type of client may be openly rude about the work, without any real agenda, and make negative comments at every possibly opportunity. This isn't your fault—they could be going through some things that they're now burdening you with, so stay professional and don't let it get you down. We've all had bad days, and your first thought should be that they may be struggling with a personal issue.

Here are some easy ways to defuse difficult situations:

* **GIVE THE CLIENT SOME SPACE:** Let them know that their reactions aren't making your work easy or helping the process. Suggest they take some time to think over the design. Often, time offers healing and clarity.

* **KILL THEM WITH KINDNESS:** Sometimes another person's passion and excitement can help someone realize they're being unhelpful.

* **BRING IN SOME CRAZY FOCUS:** Ask the client definitive questions that require a one-word answer. Do you like the color? Do you want a logo mark? Although you're not opening enough dialogue to continue the project, you're getting them to think.

ON RED FLAGS

Here are some examples of red flags to be aware of when working with clients:

- When discussing design ideas, they may say things such as, "I'll know it when I see it."
- They don't supply you with essential things you need and requested for the project, such as a design brief.
- They ask you to work the way they want, rather than allow you to use your process.

We'll never be able to effectively profile every individual we work with to figure out what they'll do and say throughout the course of a project, but as designers we can limit the damage they can cause by putting systems in place. This is another reason for "protecting the asset"—having deposits and statements of work in place allow you to relax and have clarity.

" I WILL PAY YOU AFTER THE PROJECT ONCE I KNOW WE ARE ON THE SAME PAGE. "

POTENTIAL CLIENT

" I TRUST YOUR
JUDGMENT BUT CAN IT BE
EXACTLY LIKE THIS? "

POTENTIAL CLIENT

" I CAN'T PAY YOU ANY
MONEY BUT I'LL BRING
YOU LOADS OF CLIENTS. "

POTENTIAL CLIENT

" I'M NOT SURE WHAT I
WANT BUT I'LL KNOW IT
WHEN I SEE IT. "

POTENTIAL CLIENT

" I USED TO BE A GRAPHIC
DESIGNER IN COLLEGE
BEFORE MY ACTUAL JOB. "

POTENTIAL CLIENT

" CAN YOU JUST SHOW
ME SOME SKETCHES, THEN
I'LL KNOW IF I WANT TO
WORK WITH YOU. "

POTENTIAL CLIENT

" I THINK YOU ARE A
GREAT DESIGNER—CAN
YOU MAKE MY DRAWING INTO
A LOGO. "

POTENTIAL CLIENT

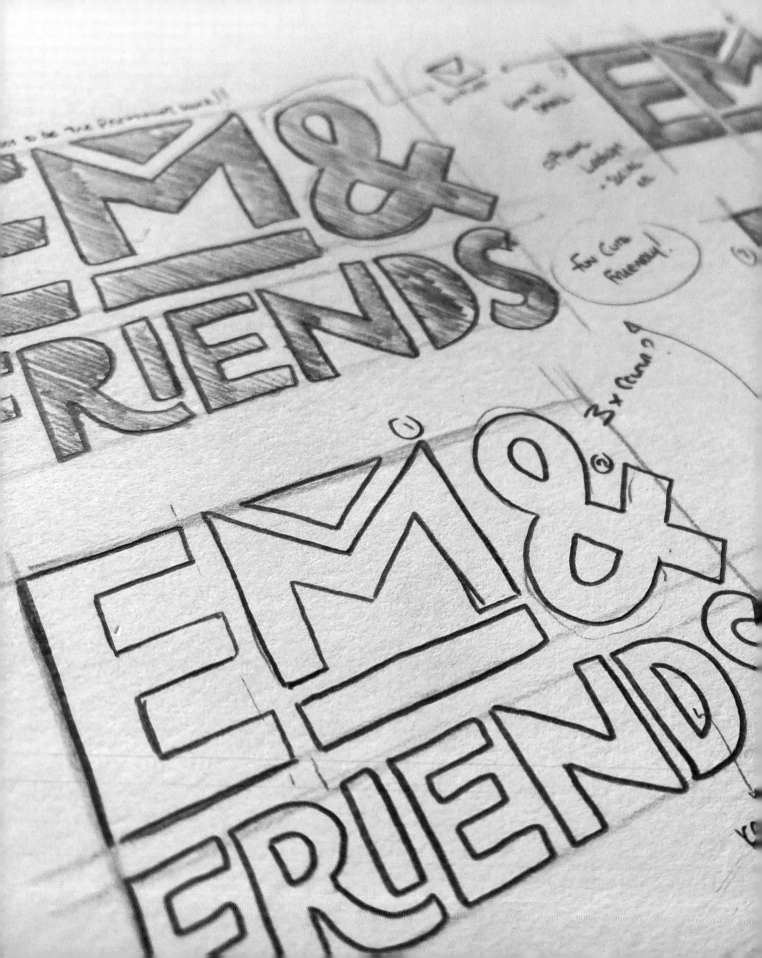

▌5 LOGO CASE STUDIES

If you've gotten this far, I can only applaud you. Your huge commitment will now be rewarded with lots of pictures and, if you're anything like me, you love a good visual.

With these case studies I want to show you how a project comes together using my process. I'll talk you through my decision making and the steps I went through to execute all these beauties that are now out in the big wide world. I've strived for variation, so there are type-based and character-based designs, along with some super-clean symbols.

These logos have stories to tell, a reason for being, and I'm eager to let you go a little further into my mind. You'll see how I've used the briefs to inform my decision making, and I'll include snippets of information from the clients and how I've communicated my ideas to them. This is going to be a lot of fun.

PLASTIC FREDM®

PLASTIC FREDM
AFTER ★ DARK

PLASTIC FREEDOM

CLIENT PROFILE: This U.K.-based online company sells a range of products from a variety of brands that are eco-friendly and plastic free. In addition, a tree is planted for every order placed. This is a one-stop-shop that makes it easy to go plastic free.

THE BACKSTORY: Out of the many logos I've created over the years, the one I did for this company is still in my top five. The high rank is probably a mixture of the plastic-free industry, the client, the free-flowing typographic style, and the freedom I was given to make something unique. Beth Noy laid out her vision for the project and gave me an excellent brief to build off. With that, I could take the design wherever I wanted.

THE CREATIVE PROCESS: While going through the process of idea generation, the most important words that came from our conversations were: knowledge, oceans, plastic free, change, freedom, organic, ethical, educate, alternatives, and planet.

These were the building blocks and values of the business that influenced my decision making, so I wanted to integrate them into the logo. I asked myself questions such as, how can I show freedom? How can I give the logo an organic feel? And how can I give the logo a human element and tie it into education?

A hand-drawn design fosters an emotional attachment to a brand, so that element was a must. The style also allowed me to celebrate the "freedom" aspect of the company's identity. Being playful with the shapes and letterforms gives the design a sense of fluidity that makes the overall look and feel very approachable and organic and also fits well with Beth's kind, fun, and free-spirited personality.

This quirky letter formation allowed me to execute two more elements I wanted to highlight: the human and educational sides of the business. While playing around with the best way to organize the letters I realized I could stack the O over the M. Adding the little smiley face to the O gave me the personable vibe I was after, and by tweaking the shape of the M I subtly visualized a book, a symbol of education and knowledge. "Om" is also a sacred sound and a spiritual symbol that signifies the essence of consciousness, and it adds value to the company's identity.

At this stage I had ticked off a few words from the list—educate, knowledge, freedom, and organic—but I still wanted to tell the story of our planet and the oceans. Instead of overcomplicating the design, I decided to work these elements into the color palette.

I chose a mixture of blue and green to express the relationship between the planet and our oceans. Using a more muted tone gives the identity a unique look while making it kind, fun, and friendly.

I've worked with Beth for almost three years now on all sorts of Plastic Freedom projects, including packaging, patterns for packaging, animations for the website and social media content, iconography, and also more logos for her podcast and side hustles. We've had a blast working together and have become good friends. Keep that in mind when you work with your next client—building relationships and friendships are valuable assets that shouldn't be ignored.

LITTLE TIP

When it comes to colors, don't be too obvious. Think abstractly and make sure the color palette you choose conforms to the company's values and isn't a random decision. Try doing some research on color theory before deciding where to land.

PIZZA REBELLION

CLIENT PROFILE: Pizza Rebellion is changing the way pizza can be served and purchased, via the U.K.'s first robotic stand-alone pizza machine that cooks a pizza in three minutes. How cool is that? The company's goal is to be established in towns and national parks across the country.

THE BACKSTORY: Everything fell into place with this project. The company that Mitch Dall and William Jack built is local to me, and I always love working with people who are part of the close community I call home. About 70 percent of the logo work I do is for clients abroad (many in the U.S., Australia, and Europe), so when a neighborhood company comes calling I get super excited. Like my Instagram bio says, "Fiercely local, but available worldwide."

THE CREATIVE PROCESS: The passion Mitch and Jack have for the company is energizing—they're big foodies and excellent businessmen. They own multiple food-based businesses in the U.K., including award-winning pubs and a traveling pizza truck, so they're no strangers to what works and what doesn't work in the food and hospitality industry.

The most important elements that needed to be featured were the speed of the pizza-making process, the pioneering approach to the way pizza is served, and the rebellious nature of the business.

The company's plan is for the containers to be placed in various parts of the U.K., so it was extremely important that the logo be legible from a distance to grab the attention of people passing by. Sticking to a bold, clean, and minimal design approach ticked these crucial boxes.

Once that was decided, I needed to make sure the design featured some semblance of a pizza, without being too obvious. I didn't want to do the standard circular pizza logo with the triangle slices. I had the chance to be rebellious and pioneering with my creativity and I wasn't going to waste the opportunity.

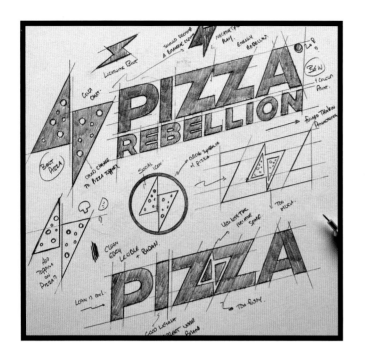

I thought about how I could show speed, energy, and all the other cool attributes this company personifies. Going through my doodle stage I started to draw lightning bolts, which epitomize speed and energy to me. I knew I was onto a winner when I simplified the shape of the bolt into two identical triangular shapes, which allowed me to visualize two pizza slices making up the lightning bolt. After adding in some pizza toppings (as circular shapes) into the triangles, I nailed my logo mark.

I like adding subtle elements to type that correlate with the logo when I can make it work. This gives the client options; they can use the type and the logo mark separately and as a whole. When playing with the ZZ shape in "pizza" I discovered I could hide another lightning bolt within the negative space. This addition is subtle but powerful in its execution.

Taking the type design a little further and being rebellious and pioneering, I gave the logo an upward slant to depict the owners' forward-thinking attitude. Knowing the logo's application and where it will be used, I took advantage of the space and placed the logo diagonally, corner to corner rather than side to side, which allowed the logo to be larger on the pizza machine containers and on the pizza boxes.

The color choices came from the brief, as always, and were directly related to my thought process for the overall concept. Going for a golden yellow relates to the energy and the lightning bolt as well as pizza's perfect golden crust. This black, gold, and white color combo makes it stand out from the competition and allows the company to be noticed.

LITTLE TIP

Don't talk like a computer when dealing with clients or potential clients. Be passionate about the work you create, and let it be heard in your voice. Allow the client to see your excitement when talking through your decision-making process. If you can't get excited about the work you're showing them, how can they?

MAIN LOGO LOCKUP - B&W

MAIN LOGO LOCKUP - COLOUR

LOGO MARK OPTIONS

UNINCORPORATED + COFFEE ROASTERS +

UNINCORPORATED COFFEE ROASTERS

CLIENT PROFILE: Unincorporated Coffee Roasters, based in Los Angeles, California, is a small but mighty brand that approaches coffee in a different way. They are playful, resilient, creative, and adaptive, and always put their customers first. The company has created an environment where people can be free, and their rogue personality is absorbing and refreshing.

THE BACKSTORY: Hands down, this is one of the coolest things I have created! In all honesty, I'm not a big fan of skull-based logos. They're so overused and difficult to make unique, purely due to the simplicity of form, shape, and the fact that a skull is a skull is a skull, if you get what I mean.

THE CREATIVE PROCESS: This project required me to rebrand the company's existing identity, which always brings a new set of challenges to the project, compared to creating a logo for a startup where there is a clean slate. I love doing rebrands, but they come with pros and cons: the fact that the company has an established voice; the owners have a deep emotional attachment to the existing logo; that change, however small, can seem dramatic—the list goes on.

I'm not going to sit here and tell you that this was an easy project; in fact, it was tough and super challenging, mainly for the reasons above. But that does not make the experience any less awesome (and rewarding) when your final design gets the all clear.

My brief was to "imagine a dead hipster who had drunk too much coffee," which sounds freaking awesome, but in the initial stages led me down a couple of dead ends (pun intended). They wanted to keep two important elements, mainly for brand recognition: the moustache and the "XX" eyes. They asked me to take these elements and add more of a rogue personality to the identity while retaining all of that awesome character.

UNINCORPORATED
COFFEE ROASTERS

UNINCORPORATED

COFFEE ROASTERS

#232323

#f4f2ed

#e8cb1f

My first attempt was a little too much of a change, although the client and I really liked it. Although the design had lots of personality it probably steered too far away from the company's personality, and the elements that needed to be incorporated were too hidden and no longer a differentiator. My second attempt brought me back to concentrating solely on the moustache and eyes, and I added some edginess and details to the elements that we needed to celebrate. This time, however, I didn't go far enough, and the client needed more.

At this stage I chatted a bit more deeply with the client and we decided to reset. He told me to ignore his ideas, and I asked for a few extra days so I could figure out my next direction with a bit more time and clarity. Sometimes when you can't nail a design the best thing to do is to take your eyes off of it for a couple of days. This always works wonders for me.

Lo and behold, on the next round I absolutely nailed it for them. Adding the element of the skull immediately added the personality they wanted. Keeping the "XX" eyes and the moustache proud and prominent kept their exiting brand alive too. The details are what make this work really well for me: the different-sized eyes that are skewed, the wonky jaw, and the added elements to the moustache. The mission was complete, and the result is something and the client and I still rave about to this day.

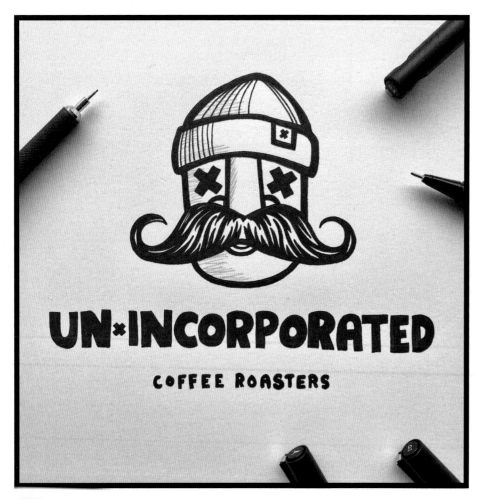

LITTLE TIP

When going through the rebranding process it's important to get a little extra detail from the client. Ask if there are any elements that need to stay, such as colors, fonts, ideas, etc. This gives you a gauge of how far you can push the design. Be sensitive to their decisions, as they may have had the design for a long time. Cushion the change.

DON CUERVO

TACO TAVERN

DON CUERVO

DON CUERVO

DON CUERVO

CLIENT PROFILE: This U.S.-based family-run Mexican restaurant has deep roots in Mexico. The dishes are made from scratch and the food is authentic.

THE BACKSTORY: When you're approached to do a logo for a company with the name Don Cuervo you drop everything, sharpen your pencils, and get ready to go crazy with creativity. Working on this logo was hands-down one of my favorite creations in 2020, and so much fun to put together.

I love this kind of project because it allows me to push myself. I enjoy creating clean and minimal monograms for my clients, but getting a brief that allows me to go in a slightly different direction gets me all fired up. Creating different identities helps me grow as a designer—I don't stick to one specific style. A logo is a logo, after all.

THE CREATIVE PROCESS: I had a clear idea of the direction I wanted to run with as soon as I finished video chatting with the company's team. Sometimes that happens, so never fight your intuition—even if it feels impulsive at times.

Straightaway I thought of imagery related to Día de los Muertos, or Day of the Dead. This holiday, celebrated in Mexico and other countries, honors family members and friends who have died. The day is more celebration than mourning, and there is something magical about that.

The festival famously features *calaveras*, which are skulls (often made of sugar) or skeletons that are colorfully dressed up and decorated. Don Cuervo loosely translates to Mr. Raven, and after a little development time and thinking, I decided to mash up a cool calavera with a raven and produced a raven's skull dressed in traditional Mexican attire. It came out fantastic.

Overthinking a solution can happen, even when ideas for a new direction are right in front of you. In this case, it was the restaurant's name. After going through a few iterations, I landed on this unique character logo, and the team loved it as much as I did.

To finish the fully customized direction in style, I carried that coolness through the typography, creating a bespoke type that worked perfectly with the logo mark. I researched classic Mexican-inspired fonts and came up with this stylized typeface. A note to logo designers: Your design shouldn't stop at the logo mark. Why not carry the design further? Going that extra mile can turn a great project into an outstanding one.

LITTLE TIP

Don't limit your research to the client's industry; take some time and look into the culture and history related to the company or brand. Those details will take your design visually to the next level and allow you to tell a more compelling story.

VEXQUISIT

CLIENT PROFILE: Vexquisit is a marketing agency that creates motion design and video production for vegan and plant-based businesses. Based in Berlin, Germany, the company's principles mirror those of their clients: respect for animals, care for the planet, and support for sustainable eating habits.

THE BACKSTORY: I love making logos for other creatives. Although the process can be challenging since you're creating designs for creative professionals, I enjoy the challenge. And if you can make another creative company happy, then you must have done a good job.

THE CREATIVE PROCESS: The words *vegan* and *plant based* are usually represented in logos by a single plant or leaf, and you can go down a design rabbit hole searching for conventional imagery. This representation is important, but I knew I could be cleverer about my thought process.

Roxy Vélez and her team are full of energy, passion, and character, and their love for animals is apparent in their everyday interactions with the world. This got me thinking about creating a cool logo based on a super-cute animal that could become a conversation starter.

During my sketch process I messed around with leaf illustrations to see if those images triggered ideas for an animal that could be integrated into the design. I realized that a leaf shape could also double as a feather. When I had my eureka moment I felt like Albert Einstein discovering the theory of relativity, only my breakthrough was that I could make a leaf into a bird.

Here's the play-by-play of how I explained my decision making to Roxy:

✱ I want the design to be simple, clever, and celebrate the happy vegan world. This logo brings energy, fun, and personality to your established brand.

✱ The logo should celebrate animals, so I created a cute and kind-looking bird image. The bird is looking back over its shoulder, making sure everyone is okay and safe—this feels on point for the company.

✱ Adding the leaf in a lighter green is a clever element and a subtle expression of love for everything plant based. It also ties into the vegan world in a unique way. I love the use of negative space and how the leaf's stem is also the bird's foot.

✱ The logo forms a V shape, another subtle win. It may not be super obvious, but some keen-eyed people will pick it up.

✱ I thought the type should be different and in tune with the fun and friendly vibe. Using all lowercase letters adds an approachable charm to the company's identity, which is clean as a whistle and extremely likable.

Breaking down the process like this makes it easier for the client to understand the information and allows them to focus on each decision I've made. I can clearly communicate what I'm showing and telling them, and they can see the full story and decision-making process.

LITTLE TIP

I like writing emails to clients similar to this bulleted play-by-play so they can easily digest the information. I used to send long, dense emails and discovered that the client missed some of the key details and theories behind my design. Keep it short and punchy.

PRINCE JAGUAR

CLIENT PROFILE: Roger Sas, also known by the stage name Prince Jaguar, is an emcee, a music producer, and an audio educator. He teaches music and assists musicians in developing their skills through educational content. He is also very spiritual and through that spirituality helps people feel motivated, grow, and heal. Roger produces, records, and engineers his own music and plays several instruments. He also uses MIDI controllers to loop and play his own beats in real time, then spits his verses on top of that. He sees hip-hop as a spiritual and artistic practice.

THE BACKSTORY: The logo mark I created for Roger is one of my most memorable—it still elicits a raw and unique energy that gives me shivers every time I look at it. He submitted a fantastic brief that outlined his mission of helping others. Roger gave me the creative freedom to interpret his brief into a logo in whatever direction my creative process would take me. Our style of working is very similar to one another—it's all about the journey and the story, so our brains were well aligned on this project.

THE CREATIVE PROCESS: Having chatted at length with Roger, it was clear he was very in tune with his spiritual beliefs and practices and that I needed to capture a "spiritual sense of belonging" with the logo direction. According to his brief, the jaguar is well rooted as a mystical and sacred animal for some indigenous tribes of Central and South America, and is still part of many of the shamanistic rituals that have survived to our age. He considers the jaguar to be his spirit animal, which he connected with during a shaman-led ceremony in Mexico.

LITTLE TIP

Always try to be in tune with your clients' needs and emotions. In creating, the logo for Prince Jaguar, words such as *spiritual* and *mystic* were key components of the design direction. Actively listening to the needs of the client will help you nail their vision.

After digesting this powerful information, I realized how important the jaguar was for Roger. When I get this vibe from a client I always lean into it hard. If I could nail the jaguar element within the design successfully, we would have a winner.

A jaguar was the obvious choice for the logo, but the execution didn't have to be obvious. I wanted to come up with clever and different ways to interpret the story. How could I take the obvious and make it unique and memorable?

After exploring a couple of different design directions, I landed on a super crazy and unique jaguar paw symbol. The claws also subtly resemble a crown, a reference to the Prince. The paw pad has an organic and free-flowing letter *P* executed within in it.

Something about this design takes it beyond a logo for me. Knowing Roger's journey, story, and mission for the future, it stands now as a symbol of positive change, one that will last forever. The design feels traveled and weathered, which taps into the powerful feeling of spirit and survival.

FUTURE BREWING

CLIENT PROFILE: This small start-up microbrewery and taproom in Sydney, Australia, plans to produce American-inspired hop-forward ales, crisp and sessionable lagers brewed in the European tradition, and lush culinary-inspired stouts. They are focused on producing high-quality, new, innovative, and exciting beers.

THE BACKSTORY: Craft brewing is an awesome and tasty industry to design for. When Brady Hannet reached out to me about doing a logo, we hit it off straight away, and talked about beer and his future plans. I've always admired the craft beer industry and see endless creative possibilities for it.

THE CREATIVE PROCESS: I'm changing things up a bit for this case study and showing you a snippet of the brief that Brady created for this project. This concise breakdown helped steer the decision making. This format is helpful if your client didn't supply a brief and you need to gather information. These questions cover the owners' backgrounds, what the company does, and the style to which they gravitate. You have a great starting point with this information alone.

Here is the snippet of the brief that Brady provided me:

* **BACKGROUND:** I have been studying brewing science and working at a craft brewery in California the past two years. I have now moved back to Sydney to open a small microbrewery and taproom in a trendy inner-city suburb with my partner, who is from the U.S.

* **FUTURE BREWING:** The name comes from my first visit to the U.S. in 2014 where my mind was blown by how advanced the country was in craft beer in terms of quality and variety. From there I knew I had to study and work in the States and bring back that knowledge and experience to the Australian market. The Future Brewing name is also about experimentation and staying ahead of the game in terms of new and exciting beer styles.

* **LOGO STYLE:** I'm looking for something modern, minimal, clean lines, fun, fresh, and hip. I would like the logo to be recognizable and stand apart from the business name. For example, for merchandise and packaged beer, I don't want it to be a beer-themed logo; it should lean more toward fashion than beer. Our target market is ages twenty-five to forty.

" I LOVE IT WHEN CLIENTS UNDERSTAND THE POWER OF BEING DIFFERENT.
"

All of this information is important, but I broke it down to the essentials that I could work with to make something epic. I wanted to create something that was a little out of the norm, since Brady said the company's name is about "staying ahead of the game in terms of new and exciting beer styles." This was my mantra as I designed the logo. I had the freedom to experiment and push the boundaries. This was all about being different, forward thinking, and staying ahead.

Here are the ideas I presented to Brady:

✴ I executed a clean, bold, and industrial-style *FB* monogram. You notice the *F* right away, but as you look closer, you'll see that the two horizontal bars of the *F* form the shape of the letter *B*, especially when you look at the negative space around the two top right elements that make up the *B*. The monogram has an ultra-modern Bauhaus style to it that gets better the more you look at it. This has longevity and will still look great in 1,000 years.

✴ The way people approach the logo parallels their attitude about the company's products. The more you explore the logo, the more elements you notice. As people drink Future Brewing beer, they start to discern more flavors and nuances. This plays on the goal of changing people's perceptions of what beer can be through new techniques and flavors within the beer-making process.

✴ Throughout the brand identity and packaging, individual elements could be used to communicate information. For example, on the monogram, imagine inserting the name "Future Brewing" on the vertical stem of the letter *F*, inserting the beer flavor or name in the horizontal bars that form the letter *B*, and the alcohol by volume (ABV) percentage in the dot. This design could be used as art, almost like masking an image. It would look awesome.

✴ The logo feels futuristic and like a new written language or alphabet, but it still communicates the brand wonderfully. The color of the circle in the bottom right could be changed to distinguish between beer genres or flavors. The logo is extremely versatile and allows for loads of fun.

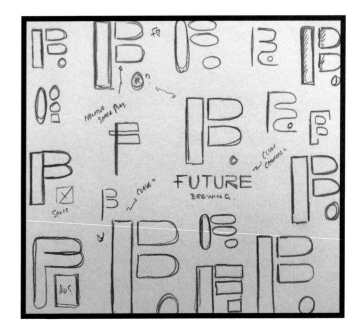

GOGO GALACTIC

CLIENT PROFILE: GOGO Galactic is a brand activation studio based in Plovdiv, Bulgaria. As a brand activation studio, they help emerging consumer brands in the U.S., EU, and U.K. build awareness for the company among their target audience.

THE BACKSTORY: I've known Lawrence Neisler, brand strategist and creative director, and Diana Kaneva, brand strategist and designer, for a number of years, and they're two of the coolest people I know and are always pushing the creative boundaries. I've worked with them on a few projects before they founded GOGO Galactic, so I consider them friends as well as clients. When they approached me to help them launch their company, I was so excited. The name alone—what's not to like?

THE CREATIVE PROCESS: I approached this project differently from the others because of my friendship and business relationship with Lawrence and Diana. They appreciate my weird and quirky way of looking at things and gave me free rein to create something cool for them. Their brief for me was simple: "Create a cool, approachable, and lovable character inspired by the name GOGO Galactic." Is that not the coolest brief ever?

So, everyone, meet MOJO from GOGO.

I can't tell you exactly how I ended up here with MOJO. In all honesty, I don't really know. I knew Lawrence and Diana loved cats, so I thought that would be a fun and memorable direction to play with—but that was as detailed as my thinking got. The rest just flowed. In your career you'll have moments when you don't need to overthink anything. Relish these opportunities and have loads of fun because they don't land on your doorstep all the time.

My mind went straight to a cat-human-alien hybrid. I visualized a planet called GOGO somewhere in the universe and imagined what the inhabitants looked like. The space theme became a creative vessel for the whole brand identity, appearing in illustrations, animations, and on the website.

LITTLE TIP

After I complete my logos I always send the client multiple types of files to cover all of their needs. Start with vector files, pngs, jpgs, and pdfs. Make sure you break elements into usable individual assets, such as logo marks and logotype.

I wanted to create a playful and quirky type that would match the character of MOJO. Drawing inspiration from the shape of planets I was able to create this bulbous, brilliant, and bespoke type style that ties the whole identity together.

When you're given an open brief by a friend, see it as an exciting opportunity rather than a lack of options. Sometimes people view the lack of a detailed brief as having no ideas to run with, but this couldn't be further from the truth with someone you know well. Once you've worked closely with someone for a while, your brains begin to align. You should always ask for some details and background on the company, but don't forget the power that freedom can bring to your creative mind. Sometimes all you need is a spark to get the creative juices flowing. Exploring ideas without boundaries is exciting. Embrace your weirdness and have fun with total freedom to create when the opportunity presents itself.

GOGO
GOGO

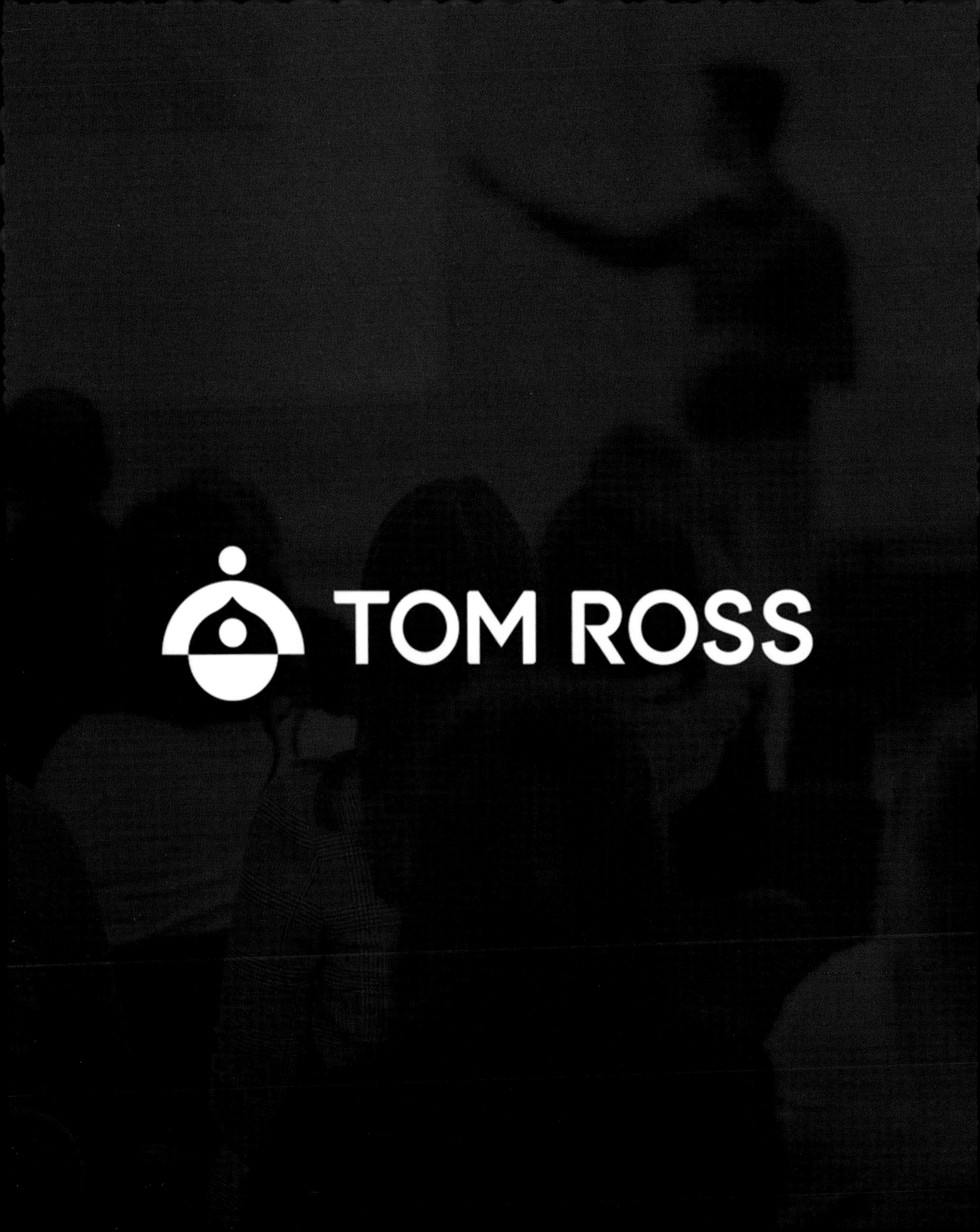
TOM ROSS

TOM ROSS

CLIENT PROFILE: Tom Ross is the CEO of Design Cuts, an online company that sells digital graphics, templates, fonts, and more. In his spare time, he teaches and mentors entrepreneurs about building engaged audiences and communities, and he's incredibly passionate about this endeavor. He's helped millions of creatives via his podcasts, The Honest Entrepreneur Show and Biz Buds (which he hosts with Mike Janda), along with social channels and live events. His greatest joy is seeing people excel in their businesses and creative pursuits.

THE BACKSTORY: Tom and I have become solid chums, and I was honored when he asked me to help him create his personal brand identity because I knew how much it meant to him and he trusted me with that responsibility.

Tom's mission is to help, support, and nurture creative entrepreneurs through his infectiously honest and caring approach. He takes the human element of branding to a new level, and we share many of the same values.

THE CREATIVE PROCESS: Tom and I chatted for an hour about his wants and needs. He is a fan of simple and clever design, so it was important to take a minimal approach with the logo. We discussed his key character points: honesty, warmth, approachability, support, and caring. Highlighting the human element of his brand was also important, since that's his superpower.

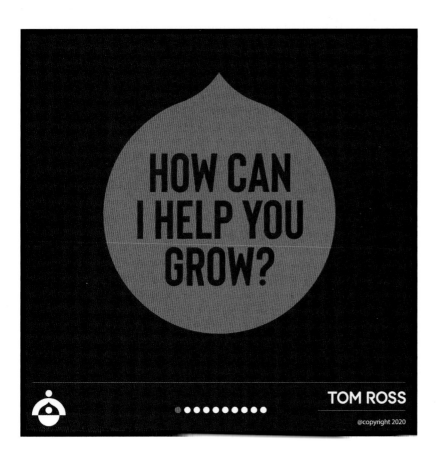

LITTLE TIP

When designing a logo, consider creating elements that can be used in a variety of ways across the brand identity. These pieces can help the client maintain a consistent brand message and better engage with their audience.

Through my standard creative process of word mapping and rapid prototyping, I created an extremely clean design that shows one human (top half) caring for another human (bottom half), which hit the key values.

I also played with the negative space to create a speech bubble between them. Tom is open to chatting with anyone and guiding them, and I wanted to communicate that idea of open and honest communication. The speech bubble "has them in it," which shows Tom chatting with people and helping them on their journey.

The logo is made out of concentric circles, a subtle but cool detail. Designed to look like a target, the grid allows me to tell his story of drilling down to your niche. Tom speaks often about the power of finding your niche as a creative. Elements can be taken out of the logo and used as marketing assets. The speech bubble element can be removed and used as a communication vessel. The circular heads can become counters, for example to allow you to see what slide number you're on in an Instagram carousel of images.

JUNGLE CULTURE

CLIENT PROFILE: Jungle Culture is a U.K.-based company that produces items from sustainable materials, such as organic coconut bowls and bamboo cutlery.

THE BACKSTORY: The owners of Jungle Culture, Chris Chalk and Jamie Skinner, asked me to create a new, hand-drawn logo and a cool pattern that could be used for all their packaging and brand identity. I love working with companies that help save the planet, and this is one of my all-time favorite projects.

THE CREATIVE PROCESS: The company sources much of its products from Vietnam, so I wanted to celebrate that connection through the logo, especially the illustrative elements in the pattern. I want the work I create to tell a story, one the client can truly relate to.

I started with the word mapping exercise (see page 79) to gather all the elements from the brief that would be beneficial to the creative process.

A bamboo shoot was an integral part of the existing logo, and my goal was to incorporate that into the new design. This is the stuff I get excited about, as it adds a new challenge to the work. At the beginning of the process I have no idea how I'm going to execute the design, but as I move through the steps of my process and develop ideas, opportunities for execution present themselves. Understanding that the logo needed to be seamlessly transferred onto multiple items, I knew the design needed to be compact. I stacked the words, placing "Jungle" on top of "Culture." This would allow the logo to work in smaller spaces and be more versatile for the client.

By stacking the words, I was able to use one big letter *U* for *Jungle* and *Culture*. I love playing with negative space when the opportunity presents itself, and after positioning the *U*, I knew right away I could add the bamboo design into that shape.

LITTLE TIP:

Always think about the applications for a logo. Where will it be used? What materials will it be printed on? What color will it be primarily printed on? What size variations are needed? These are all key considerations in executing the design.

Knowing a smaller icon may be needed, I created a couple of options of the *JC* monogram with the added bamboo leaves from the main logo. I love the hand-drawn organic feel of this logo, and the ragged edges of the font make the logo appear grounded and earthy.

I was also asked to create a bespoke pattern for use on packaging materials and merchandise, with the individual elements of the design available for social media and website icons, etc. In the first iteration I went generic tribal, which didn't accurately tell the story of Vietnam. I researched Asian art, specifically from the Vietnamese culture, and learned about the Chim Lac (a mythical bird symbol) and other icons of Vietnam's history and ancient cultural heritage. After this development, exploration, and guidance from the owners, we ended up with this beautiful design.

The color palette adds a little punch and vibrancy to the brand identity that will help the company stand out long into the future. This combination felt fresh, while retaining the cool jungle feeling. What an honor it was to be a part of this.

BRAND FOCUSED
DESIGN-LED

WE FOSTER CREATIVITY, INDIVIDUALITY AND PLACE YOUR BRAND
AT THE HEART OF CONVERSATION.

PRINT / BRAND / WEB / MOTION

6 GROWTH AND LONGEVITY

I've noticed something weird among some designers in our industry: a serious lack of patience and skewed priorities. People are focused on gaining social media followers and likes rather than gaining clients and nurturing existing relationships. When this get-rich-quick mentality doesn't happen, they move on to something else.

Good things take time. We live in a world that moves quickly. Remember that you're in charge of your own destiny. In this world, patience is power. Trying a career path for two years and not getting anywhere is pretty normal. If you interviewed ten top designers and asked how long it took them to find their feet in the industry, they likely would say a minimum of two years.

I've been in the industry for fifteen years, but I think I have another thirty years of awesomeness still to come. Key attributes of any designer are keeping things simple, not overthinking, persevering through hard times, and being open to change.

Always play the long game, as it gives your short-term productivity real clarity.

"EFFORT IS FREE."

BEING PROLIFIC AND CONSISTENT

I used to be prolific and consistent at being an idiot. The day I started Baby Giant with Ady that all changed. I needed to show up daily to make it a success and bring bucketloads of effort. The idiot in me still shows himself every now and again (it only tends to happen on weekends), but at least he has some structure.

Putting effort into something costs nothing. As soon as you harness that power, you'll find that you'll be more productive and become more creative with your ideas. Putting effort into drawing every day will make you better at drawing, putting effort into reading business strategy books will give you a better understanding of business, and putting effort into marketing yourself will bring in more clients.

Effort needs to be a priority. You need to allocate your efforts to activities that reap the biggest rewards and help you long into the future. I put most of my effort into these areas:

* **FORMULATING GOOD HABITS**

* **MAINTAINING A CLEAR AND STRUCTURED ROUTINE**

* **PERFECTING MY PROCESS**

Since effort is free, it's easy to give it away to nonessentiall tasks. I suggest you think big and constantly ask yourself whether the effort you're putting in to an activity is the best use of your time.

Could you spend two hours working on your drawing skills instead of scrolling through social media? Could you read a book on business instead of watching your favorite Netflix series? Every time I start an activity, I ask myself, is this a good use of my time? If the answer is no, I apply my efforts to something else.

Being prolific and consistent happens when you apply effort to things that matter. Once you know what you want to be, put a plan together outlining how you can make yourself the most efficient human possible. Trim the nonessentials and double down on the practices that will help you carve out a long and successful career. Simplicity is a key factor in this, so clarifying what needs to be improved is the best way to focus your effort. Effort equals reward.

LITTLE TIP

Write down three things that you want to improve in your life. For the next year put effort into working on them. This time next year you will have made a huge amount of progress.

▌ THE SELF-DOUBT JACKAL

Occasionally I'm approached by young designers who are trying to find their way in the world. Instead of barraging them with short, punchy, actionable tips via direct messages or email, I'll suggest a chat to hash out some ideas.

One of these calls was with a designer named Caitlyn. She came across as fun, comfortable, and easy to talk to, so I was surprised to hear she struggled with confidence when presenting herself, her work, and her prices to her clients. She called this lack of confidence "The Jackal."

I lacked self-assurance early in my career too, and I'm sure many of you reading this have struggled with your own creative jackal. I've outlined a few techniques to help you gain confidence in your work, some easy practices, and a few activities you can implement into your day.

* **FIND AN HONEST FRIEND:** If we're lucky, we have that one friend we can turn to for the unfiltered truth. These people are valuable as they constantly tell you what they honestly think. When you have an idea or a piece of finished work, send it to them for comments before sending it to anyone else. Ask them to be brutally honest. This process will help you gain confidence when receiving good and bad feedback and will prepare you for the world.

* **TEMPORARILY SHARE YOUR WORK:** Putting our work out into the world can seem daunting, especially when it may be there for many years to come. Instead, practice temporary sharing. Share something publicly for a day or a week, making sure you're in control of the duration. The challenge of sharing is easier when you know you have the power to remove a piece of work after a day. I guarantee that after a while you'll gain confidence in your own work and leave it untouched.

* **READ BOOKS ON THE AREAS YOU STRUGGLE WITH:** This seems so obvious, but I wonder how many of you do no research on the subjects you struggle with. Seeking knowledge around your troubles can begin to paint a picture, since our insecurities often stem from other events. Understanding the catalyst will help define the answers.

Over time your jackal with lose its power. Remember that self-doubt is natural and happens to everyone. Be brave and take it at your own pace. Your courage will grow along with your confidence.

"SIMPLICITY IS NOT LAZINESS."

▍ KEEP IT SIMPLE

Before I started Baby Giant I was a full-stack designer, which translated into "pretty average at everything." I was trying to be everything to everybody, and it had a negative effect on my creativity. I learned that as your career progresses you should narrow your offerings and services so you can become an expert in your field.

Sometimes that process is referred to as developing a business or professional niche, which means serving a specific area of a larger market. In the early years of your creative career you shouldn't niche down to a specific discipline—but you should do it eventually. Focusing on a niche creates an amazing amount of clarity, and clarity brings focus. When you focus on an individual niche, it becomes very clear how to get better at it and how to find clients. Simplifying your services and serving a particular part of an industry allows you to engage with the right audience and attract the right clients.

You should also be implementing simplicity throughout your life, not just for business. I have streamlined everything I do, which allows me to concentrate my time and energy on the most important tasks and people. I don't have a massive group of friends, but the people I do spend time with always get 100 percent of my attention. My weekends are mostly spent relaxing and re-energizing. Just because you have the space to do something doesn't mean you have to fill it.

Simplicity is not laziness. Simplifying your life and work will really help you be more effective and productive in the elements you have chosen to keep.

LITTLE TIP

When you create a to-do list for the day, make sure you circle the most important tasks. Getting the most important things completed first will reduce stress levels and help bring focus to what's important.

SURROUND YOURSELF WITH THE RIGHT PEOPLE

When I was a teenager I had a group of friends that weren't a good influence on me, but I also believe that I was not a good influence on them either. We were all young and enjoyed doing the same things. As individuals we were nice people, but as a group the dynamic changed and became toxic. Eventually we were expelled from school, and I went down a path of wasting time for another two or three years—time I will never get back.

The process of growing up is often the catalyst for creating the right relationships. Over time you'll naturally gravitate toward people who have a similar mindset and believe in the same things you do. If you're open to change and make an effort to better yourself, you'll be rewarded. I'm a big believer in the idea that you receive the energy you put out into the world, so being positive and kind will attract upbeat and friendly people.

Imagine spending time with someone who is constantly whining and negative; that would no doubt start to rub off on you. Now, imagine spending time with someone who is positive and happy all the time—the effect on your mood would be awesome. If you want to make something of yourself, it helps to be around people with a similar drive. They will keep you motivated and accountable and help you succeed.

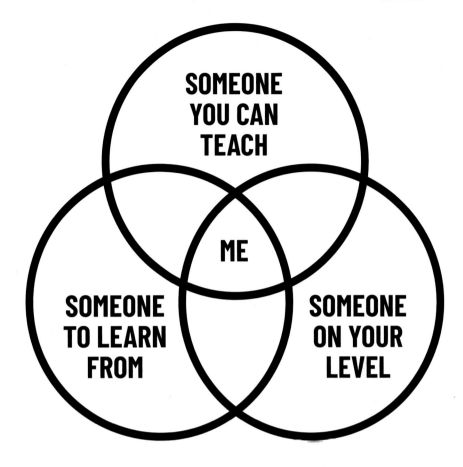

SOMEONE YOU CAN TEACH

ME

SOMEONE TO LEARN FROM

SOMEONE ON YOUR LEVEL

MY THREE TYPES OF PEOPLE

Surround yourself with these three types of people and you'll always be growing as a human: someone you can teach, a peer or colleague, and someone you can learn from. You don't have to limit this to three people, but the idea behind this theory is powerful.

* **SOMEONE YOU CAN TEACH:** Sharing knowledge is an important part of life, so passing on what we've learned helps others grow. We become better communicators and we learn the importance of humility.

* **SOMEONE ON YOUR LEVEL:** Being able to chat often with someone who understands who you are and what you do is vital. You can keep each other motivated and accountable.

* **SOMEONE YOU CAN LEARN FROM:** Learning throughout life is a superpower. As soon as you think you know everything you might as well give up. Choose a businessperson, a favorite author, or someone you admire on social media.

The people you select don't have to be in your industry, especially friends and colleagues and those you want to learn from. Being able to absorb and share knowledge from other perspectives and industries is a fantastic asset and helps you approach life more holistically.

█ STAY CURIOUS

If you think you have something figured out and you no longer have to work at your career because you're the most talented human on the planet, then you have lost.

Surrounding yourself with people you can learn from is a huge part of your personal development. Don't take this too literally—there is this wonderful thing called the Internet and these amazing things called books, so you don't have to be face to face with someone to gain their knowledge and insights.

If I could choose one word to describe me in the last five years, it would be curious. Getting up early and reading is one of the single best habits I practice. In the last three years I've learned more before 6:30 a.m. than I have in my whole life, and it comes down to one thing: my insatiable curiosity. I love discovering new things, reading different perspectives, and learning from completely different people, in vastly different industries. I've read books on philosophy, history, self-care, establishing habits, and psychology, and each book has helped me advance personally and professionally.

I used to talk a lot, but now I listen. I absorb how the industry is moving, hear different perspectives from people I chat with, and make sure I don't pigeonhole myself as an influencer, or whatever you want to call it.

I've never wanted to be defined by a logo club or influencer club. You lose the ability to think bigger when you create boundaries or define yourself too narrowly. I know I niche my career, but I don't want to niche my thinking.

Today it's far too easy to tailor what you hear, watch, and interact with. Technology has turned the world into a manufactured algorithm that shows us what we want to see. I urge you to look deeper and explore ideas that go against your views and opinions. I need to do more of that, too. Stay curious.

"I KNOW I NICHE MY CAREER, BUT I DON'T WANT TO NICHE MY THINKING."

SLEEP A LOT, PLAY A LOT

The creative industry is different from other professions. Our brains need to perform at high levels and, at times, in a different way from those in other professions. We create visual experiences that must communicate well and hold the viewer's attention. This isn't easy, even in the best of times.

In order to work at our peak, we need to focus on two key areas: sleep and play. I've been working on prioritizing these two essentials, since they're integral to my development as a creative.

SLEEP FOR CREATIVES

Lack of sleep has been linked to poor brain function, and mood swings and massively contributes to the mistakes we make. Getting adequate sleep allows you to think more clearly and makes you more efficient. Getting ample sleep improves problem-solving and decision-making skills and should be a priority. Don't see sleep as wasting time; see it as an asset to productivity.

PLAY FOR CREATIVES

The ability to play and have fun makes us more creative, even though as adults we're often told not to play. Allowing the brain space to explore without constraints lets us see the world a little differently. This is a benefit for creatives. Always think: What would the five-year-old me do?

Sleep and play are just as important as developing drawing and software skills. To be able to perform to the best of our ability, we need to recharge and playfully explore. Building these fundamentals into your daily routine and making them a priority ensures a long, fun, and well-rested career. I guarantee your productivity will increase.

▌7 RUDE NOT TO CONCLUDE

I was an absolute waste of space when I was in my teens. I never finished anything properly—except for a keg of beer—so if you don't mind, I'm going to give myself a high five, since this book has been an absolute pleasure to write and finish.

Please send me a picture that I can share with the world. This book would never have happened without you. Tag me on Instagram (@made.by.james) or email me: james@madebyjames.co. We're a part of each other's journey now, and that needs to be shared.

I didn't want this book to just be about idea creation and logo design; I also wanted it to be about sustaining and caring for your creativity. I hope some of the tips and techniques you've learned will serve you well in the future. Our habits and routines play as important a role as our ability to draw and communicate. Our logo creation process is just as vital as our process for relaxing after work.

This rectangular stack of paper will be your best friend throughout your creative career. If you're struggling to come up with ideas, have a difficult client, or are in need of a friend to talk to, this book is here for you.

▌ TAKEAWAYS

I could keep writing forever, but I am only allowed so many words. I've kept the information as precise as possible, and I've tried to limit my general rambling to a minimum. With that in mind, I'd like to distill the main points even further with five key takeaways.

Think of these as little slices of pizza that you can easily devour and enjoy, and see them as a recap that can prompt you to remember the valuable information you want to take into your life.

If you remember these five beauties you will be the creative badass I know you can be:

✳ **THINK ABOUT JOB TEN, NOT JUST JOB ONE:** Build long-lasting relationships and take time to get to know the people you work with. Nurturing an existing relationship is much easier than finding a new one. Build trust, communicate openly, and go the extra mile for your client. If you look after them, they'll look after you. Remember to bring your personality to the table and embrace the human element of design.

✳ **PROCESS, PROCESS, PROCESS:** Work hard at your creative practice and always remain in control of your work. Never stop tweaking your process and continue to evolve the way you work and communicate. A solid process will be your friend in the good times and the bad. Let your clients know your work methods right from the start, and never stray from that. The client has come to you because you're the expert. Remember to watch out for those red flags when working with someone new.

✳ **YOU CAN'T DO IT ALL:** Consider the power of collaboration and the money you can make as the facilitator. Say yes to everything within reason and find people who will help complete projects you can't do yourself. Be the person clients calls when they need something. Surround yourself with the right people and don't be afraid to ask for help. Partner with other talented humans and build a network of awesomeness. Your creative skills are more important than your administrative skills. Releasing some control will give you longevity in the industry.

✳ **NEVER STOP LEARNING:** Remain curious and open to new challenges. When you think you know everything, you might as well stop. Pushing for more knowledge will help you become a true leader. Research your industry and others. Consistently growing your knowledge base will help you long into the future.

✳ **BE YOURSELF:** Being authentic is the most difficult thing a person can do, but it's the most powerful asset you have. There's only one you. Don't compare yourself to anyone else and enjoy the freedom that being yourself can bring to your professional and personal lives. Being yourself is much easier than trying to be someone else. You'll attract the right people like a magnet and never have to hide in the darkness. Shine brightly, my friends. You are here for a reason. The world needs you.

JAMES MARTIN - 15 YEARS

I'M JUST GETTING STARTED

40-YEAR CAREER

BE PATIENT WITH YOURSELF

This point could have been number six on the list, but I wanted to make it a bigger deal. Patience is the one thing that stops people from reaching their true potential. We all develop at different speeds—I created my first logo when I was about twenty-five, and before that I was an idiot who thought the world owed me something.

A successful career doesn't happen overnight. It takes time to grow into a fully functioning machine of creative awesomeness. It takes time to build a client base, and that is true for everyone. The people you look up to have put in many years of hard work and struggled along the way. They made it because they were patient with themselves.

A huge amount of patience is needed to know what you want to do in life. Ignore the noise about growing 100,000 social media followers in six months. All of that is ego based and not sustainable. Plus, who cares about beating the algorithm?

Spend your early years taking time to grow and explore. Why give up after two years? If we're lucky, we have about a forty-year career span in any chosen industry. There's no need to rush or hack your way to the top of the creative pyramid. As with any business, you have to earn your stripes, and when you see progress you'll know it's well deserved through hard work and effort.

Look after yourself and be patient with yourself. You will not regret it.

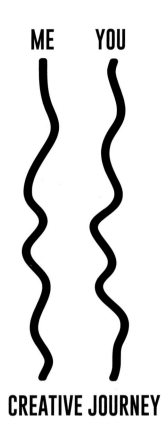

ME   YOU

CREATIVE JOURNEY

▌ENJOY THE JOURNEY

This little part of our journey together is coming to a close, and I must admit, it's been an absolute blast chatting with you. There is no straight path in life—well, not that I've found—but that's what makes it so interesting and never boring. You will hit hurdles, have hardships, and experience pain along the way, but you will also find love, friendship, and opportunities you never thought possible.

The journey I've shared in this book has been filled with mistakes, pain, luck, trauma, wins, losses, positives, negatives, and most importantly, red crayons. I'm sure the coming years will be mostly the same; in the next chapter I'll be slightly more in control because of what I've learned, and I've shared that with you in this book.

Enjoy the process of figuring yourself out, learning new things, building flourishing relationships, and, last but not least, becoming a badass creative who uses their skills to help others. You will never have it all figured out, so embrace change with open arms and enjoy the journey of becoming you. And never let anyone tell you you're not good enough.

My mate Beth from Plastic Freedom asked me this question during her podcast: "If you could go back in time and give your younger self one piece of advice, what would it be?"

I said, "I would tell myself not to change a thing."

MBJ
Made
BY JAMES

▌RESOURCES

Favorite design podcast

✱   Logo Geek podcast with Ian Paget: logogeek.uk/podcast/

✱   Perspective Podcast with Scotty Russell: perspective-collective.com/perspectivepodcast/

✱   The honest designers podcast: www.honestdesigners.com

Favorite designers who motivate me

✱   Michael Janda: @morejanda

✱   Scotty Russell: @coachscottyrussell

✱   Jessica Walsh: @jessicavwalsh

✱   Roberta Hall: @happyimpulse

✱   Mario Quezada: @themarioquezada

✱   Lincoln Design Co: @lincolndesignco

Favorite non-designers who motivate me

✱   Gary Vaynerchuk: @garyvee

✱   Brené Brown: @brenebrown

✱   Tom Ross: @tomrossmedia

Favorite design resources

✱   Set Sail Studios: @setsailstudios

✱   Studio Innate: @studioinnate

✱   Design Cuts: @designcuts

Favorite artists

✱   Adam Issac Jackson: @adamisaacjackson

✱   Timmy Ham: @iamsloth

✱   Danielle Weber: @daniellesartwork

Favorite logo designers

✱   Paula Scher of Pentagram: @ paula_scher_; @pentagramdesign

✱   Aaron Draplin: @draplin

✱   George Bokhua: @george_bokhua

There are many more people I could (and probably should) have added to this list, but I needed to keep it short. The world is full of powerful and brilliant people who can inspire you every day, so go seek them out, say hi, and involve yourself in their world.

Also, don't forget to hit up my website, themadebyjames.com, for all things logo design, including courses, coaching, and resources. If you want to be a badass logo designer, then come and get involved.

▌ACKNOWLEDGMENTS

Like all of us, we are a sum of our parts, and this opportunity would not have happened without every single person I've met or crossed paths with. But there are a few people I really need to give some love to.

John and Susie Martin, a.k.a. mum and dad: thank you for always teaching me the difference between right and wrong, even if in the early years I never listened. Thank you for your constant support and for always allowing me to explore my weird and wonderful world without judgment.

Chris Martin, a.k.a. bro: thanks for being a friend in good times and bad and always keeping my competitive spirit high, even if it did end with us chasing each other around the garden and throwing cricket stumps at one another.

Kate Martin, a.k.a. wifey: you have always been my biggest cheerleader, and on top of that you're my best friend. Thank you for keeping me grounded and always being yourself. That power you have has helped me be okay with who I am.

Adrian Matengu, a.k.a. Ady: my man, it's been a long ride, and we still have a long way to go. I appreciate your friendship, guidance, and the fact that you always stick with me and my crazy ideas. Here's to the next decade.

Nicky O'Dell-Shearn, a.k.a. my sister from another mister: you were the kick up the arse I needed, and without you I don't feel this book would have ever happened. Thanks for always telling me that I was good enough and that I could always be more. Your friendship means the world to me.

▌ABOUT THE AUTHOR

James Martin, also known as Made by James, is an award-winning brand identity designer and cofounder of Baby Giant Design Co. He grew up being creative, developed his skills in illustration, became a teacher, then a tattoo artist apprentice, and has been in the graphic design world for fifteen years. His knowledge and unique outlook allow him to thrive in a competitive design industry.

James's willingness to share his creative process, offer honest advice, and engage with fans and followers on social media have earned him a reputation as a generous and wise mentor and inspiration, especially to junior designers and those just getting started in the field. His clients include music industry heavy hitters The Chainsmokers, Michael Ray, and Carter McLean as well as brands such as Em & Friends, Pizza Rebellion, and Plastic Freedom.

▮ INDEX